Trans-Dime Communication

Tales of a Battery-Powered Psychic Medium

Roderick Millington

A Dark Side of the Moon Publication

For Diane

A Heavenly Postcode

"Being a medium who can communicate with souls isn't the same as one who can interact with them. It's the difference between listening in on a conversation and changing the subject."
Kelley Harrell, Teen Spirit Guide to Modern Shamanism

I am not clairvoyant, I can't channel, and I'm not a healer; I can't see auras, read palms, or clear chakras. Even so, I do talk to the so-called 'dead'. Furthermore, every communication is recorded and saved on my computer. Because the one thing I can do, as long as the battery on my laptop is sufficiently charged, is Trans-Dimensional Communication (TDC); that is, enjoy two-way conversations with the spirit world.

TDC (a close cousin of EVP – Electronic Voice Phenomenon) is an observable fact that many prominent people have studied. It is incredibly fascinating and just a tiny bit against the laws of the universe. During telephone communications, radio broadcasts, and while recording on computers and other modern technology, voices appear for which there is no rational explanation.

Dr Peter Bander, a senior lecturer at the Cambridge Institute of Education, was a trained psychologist and Christian theologian who had a great aversion to psychic phenomena. He went as far as to say that the mere idea that the dead could communicate with the living was not only far-fetched; it was outrageous. As a result, when publisher Colin Smythe asked him to help investigate EVP in 1972, he said, "Thanks, but no thanks."

1

However, Smythe decided to experiment independently, using the procedures outlined in Konstantin Raudive's pioneering book, 'Breakthrough'. He then asked Bander to listen to one of his tapes. The stony-faced sceptic sat like a statue for ten minutes, and then the colour drained from his face. "I noticed the peculiar rhythm mentioned by Raudive and his colleagues ... I heard a voice ... I believe this to be the voice of my mother who died three years earlier," Bander explained.

Bander's life had taken a complete 180-degree swing, and he began to conduct his own tests under the most stringent of controls. On one very well known occasion, the EVP experiments were conducted in soundproofed studios to eliminate stray sounds and filter out stray broadcasts. Approximately two hundred voices were picked up in the space of just twenty-seven minutes, making converts of the disbelieving Pye sound engineers who supervised the session.

In Bander's subsequent book, 'Voices from the Tapes', he quotes Pye's chief engineer, Ken Attwood, saying: "I have done everything in my power to break the mystery of the voices without success; the same applies to other experts. I suppose we must learn to accept them." Another highly respected recording professional, Ted Bonner of Decca and RTE, said: "This is no trick. This is no gimmickry; this is something we have never dreamed of before."

Bander, as we have seen, was a committed Christian, and this alone caused him at first to reject the evidence without even hearing it. Rigid belief like this is quite a common Christian trait. Sadly, people who have made up their minds about something rarely listen to other viewpoints. Bander is to be commended, then, for listening and having the courage to accept a new reality.

You would perhaps expect the Catholic Church to proclaim this type of work as being influenced by the devil. And it can appear that way on the surface. Yet two of the earliest EVP investigators were Italian Catholic priests, Father Ernetti and Father Gemelli.

The two priests discovered EVP through a twist of fate in 1952 when they were recording Gregorian chants. Father Gemelli heard the voice of his father on the tape calling him by a childhood nickname: "Zucchini, it is clear, don't you know it is I?"

Profoundly troubled by Catholic teachings concerning communication with the deceased, the two priests visited Pope Pius XII in Rome, hoping, no doubt, for clarification at best and exorcism at worst. The Pope surprised them both with his answer: "Dear Father Gemelli, you really need not worry about this. The existence of this voice is strictly a scientific fact and has nothing to do with spiritism. The recorder is totally objective. It receives and records sound waves from wherever they come. This experiment may perhaps become the cornerstone for building scientific studies which will strengthen people's faith in the hereafter."

The Vatican then permitted other priests to conduct their own experiments. Father Leo Schmid, a Swiss theologian, collected more than ten thousand voices, the transcripts of which he published in his book, 'When the Dead Speak'.

Archbishop H.E. Cardinale, Apostolic Nuncio to Belgium, commented: "Naturally, it is all very mysterious, but we know the voices are there for all to hear them."

The Vatican continues to sponsor wide-ranging research into all areas of parapsychology, including EVP/TDC. In 1997, Father Gino Concetti, one of the most accomplished theologians in the Vatican, said in an interview with the Vatican newspaper, Osservatore

Romano: "According to the modern catechism, God allows our dear departed persons, who live in an ultra-terrestrial dimension, to send messages to guide us in certain difficult moments of our lives. The Church has decided not to forbid anymore the dialogue with the deceased with the condition that these contacts are carried out with a serious religious and scientific purpose."

EVP/TDC has progressed enormously since the days of reel-to-reel and cassette tape recording, and these days a mind-to-mind etheric link is often created between the human plane and the non-physical plane. The psychic medium is the instrument through which this occurs, combining natural psychic gifts with technology to allow TDC to happen. This is how I work. It is a spiritual endeavour that seeks to validate, comfort, heal and encourage. It is a gift from beyond.

When I listen to a TDC recording, I focus not only on white and ambient noise but also on the human voice, both forward and in reverse. Spirit modulates and modifies this noise matrix to produce comments and responses. Even a cough, something being dropped, or a door opening, can be modulated. Because of this, I find voices appearing out of background noise and 'riding on the back' of the human voice. Voices are also heard where there is total silence - no one is talking, and there is no background noise - and in some cases, they speak over the top of people holding a conversation.

I discovered my first voice during the summer of 2004, when the world, I assumed I knew, began to change without warning, and another world started to overlap with reality. Emerging from the speakers of my laptop, I heard my father, who had passed away two years earlier, announce, *"Thank God, I walk without them pills."* This was astounding on many levels, yet I had to accept it as

4

real because I could hear it, and ultimately, because it was recorded, so could my family and friends.

It was a statement that made perfect sense, too. For quite some time before his death, my father needed to take a whole pharmacy of prescription drugs first thing each morning just to be able to function. He had chronic rheumatoid arthritis, heart failure, and other assorted medical curiosities. When he was rushed into hospital exactly a week before he died, the doctor there was disgusted with the number of pills my father's GP had given him, which most likely contributed to his demise. So yes, pills were a massive part of my father's daily life, and he hated it. Therefore, looking back, having got over the initial shock of actually hearing 'the voice', the fact that he made that statement was logical; it's what he would say to make me understand that it was him talking.

When you hear a voice from another world, you naturally want more! That is an innate human response. Would I be able to repeat what, for me, was a minor miracle? Well, it was quite a few weeks of challenging and not very successful work, but eventually, it paid off.

Sitting in front of my laptop, following the same steps I had when I received the 'pills' message, I tried asking my father a few questions to see if I could pick up another voice. It seemed like something of a long shot, but one September evening, I heard my father speak once again.

I had asked him for the name of someone from his past, maybe someone with whom he went to school. I further emphasised that it had to be information that I was not aware of. Almost immediately upon playing back the recording, I discovered a message I did not understand but was probably checkable. At this time, my mother was still alive, so I played her the recording I had found relating to a possible friend or relative of my father, *"Father remembers Beryl."*

5

My mother's smile broadened in approval; she loved anything to do with the supernatural, "Yes, Beryl was a big friend of your dad. He used to go to school with her. She married his closest friend, Dennis." I had not dared hope that this could be true, and when I found out it was, it pretty much took my breath away.

I immediately wanted to ask my father many more questions, and following the 'Beryl' TDC, I felt much more confident of obtaining a result.

First, I decided to ask about my uncle, Eric, who had passed away in 1985. Eric had come forwards a few years before on only my second ever visit to a spiritualist church. "Excuse me, but do you know anyone by the name of Eric?" the platform medium asked me. I was a bit like a rabbit caught in headlights, and at first, I didn't know whether I did. Then she added, "He is no longer with us; he passed over many years ago."

That gave me enough to time gather my thoughts, and I said, "Yes, I used to know an Eric. He was my uncle." "Oh," she responded, "well, he's telling me about a factory." A shiver went down my spine. Before his sudden death in 1985, Eric, my father's brother, had built up a considerable business and had spent his entire working life in a factory.

"Are you in the medical profession, perhaps a nurse?" "No, I have no connection to the healthcare world - apart from being an occasional patient," I replied weakly. "Well," she began, "Eric is showing you surrounded by nurses."

At the time, being told that I was, or would be, surrounded by nurses made no sense. Two years later, though, my father died in hospital, and six years after that, my mother died in a nursing home. Consequently, I was indeed 'surrounded' by nurses for several years – my mother, after her two strokes, lived for a further two and a half years, the majority of which were in hospitals and nursing homes. The warning I had been given had undoubtedly come true, even if on the night in question, it meant nothing.

I had always liked Eric, and as I sat recording yet another conversation with my invisible father, I said so. I discussed Eric because I was curious about whether my father had met up with his brother in the afterlife. I quickly found out that he had. *"Eric's up here with me,"* was the message I picked up.

But where exactly was 'up here'? Heaven? Does such a place exist? Of course, we can't 'prove' it one way or another, and it's a concept I have always had trouble with. Oh, I'm quite happy to believe in an afterlife, but an actual 'place' called Heaven sounds a little like a celestial Bourton-on-the-Water. I guess my idea was a little more abstract and possibly something that I could not understand on this side of an intensive care unit.

Nevertheless, if there was a Heaven, I wanted to know what they did there, so I asked. *"For me, it must now go easy - he needs help,"* was the instant response. There appeared to be two entities communicating; first, my father (for me, it must now go easy) and then a second 'person' (he needs help). He was exhausted when he passed on, there's no question about that, and nothing but rest can cure exhaustion. Physiological rest is the most crucial remedy for treating all ailments. And since all ailments derive from exhaustion of one type or another, rest, both physical and emotional, is the most potent of all remedies. Moreover, it would appear that this is as true in 'Heaven' as it is in Liverpool, Milan, or Philadelphia.

At first, this sounds slightly odd. My father no longer had a body, so why would he need to rest. Well, perhaps because his physical body had gone downhill so dramatically over the last decade of his life, this had had a severe impact on his emotional and, yes, spiritual wellbeing. Bearing this in mind, maybe it is not such a big surprise that he would need to rest on the other side.

Right at the end of this particular recording session, I suddenly felt a presence in the room, and 'electricity' started to flow through my body. Intuitively, I felt my father was close, and in voicing this opinion, I received the following response, *"My hands work, hear me, Rick."* Rheumatoid arthritis, it appeared, was no longer a problem.

I was not too surprised that my father was able to communicate; he not only had a tenacity that allowed him to get things done, he was also a little psychic, a spiritual gift that seemed to have followed him into the heavenly realms.

He was a former Royal Navy officer and engineer who, while generally open-minded, had a tendency to call a spade a spade. During the latter part of his career, he found himself in China working on a large project in what was once known as Manchuria. While there, he woke up early one morning, about 5.00 am, he said, to a "Chinaman laid out in old-fashioned clothes on the bed next to mine." Who was this man, and why was my father seeing him? Like most paranormal puzzles, there is no answer to this, but the 'dead' Chinese man disappeared from view after around a minute.

My father took all of this in his stride. He had previously experienced similar paranormal encounters, including hearing the voice of a former co-worker over the factory loudspeaker on the day he died, but before anyone knew he had died.

I will also share an experience that happened just a week or so before his death, in August 2002. "I had a very odd experience last night," he started to tell me. "I woke up, and standing beside the bed was a man dressed in a two-piece suit and crewneck sweater, all green. He was looking at me and holding a knife."

A dream? Maybe I would have thought so, too, if it wasn't for the fact that a few years earlier, I had a similar experience, but this one was a dream. There was a party in a house, and I was upstairs. However, I suddenly felt that my father was in trouble, and I 'floated' quickly down the stairs and walked into the lounge. My father was sitting in an armchair at one end of the room. At the other end, a man stood dressed in a two-piece suit and crewneck sweater, all black. He was looking at my father and holding a knife. I moved between the two of them and puffed myself up like a cat to stop the man from throwing the knife. There the dream ended. Yet the man sounded the same except for the colour of the clothes, one green and one black.

My father's TDC communications set in motion the beginning of an extraordinary and fascinating journey for me. I have now recorded thousands of voices - deceased friends, family, guides, and other entities. And I am delighted to continue working with Spirit in the hope that I can help people recognise that they are more than their physical bodies. In today's secular world, most people, when they look at the cold, barren, and technologically led landscape, find it hard to sense any life outside of their own immediate experience. Yet whenever a much-loved family member is no longer alive, they have to deal with unimaginable pain and sorrow without any spiritual support. It was not supposed to be like this, and I find such widespread ignorance and denial shocking.

People often ask where the voices come from? I say 'Heaven' only because that's what the spirit communicators call it. The first time I got word of Heaven was after communicating with my father for the first time. My father frequently refers to me as 'Rick' when getting in touch with me through TDC - it's a name he called me regularly over the initial ten years of my life, then for reasons unknown, I became 'Rod'. However, I was called Rick once more when I found a 'message' on my computer.

This other voice calling me Rick was discovered on Real Player One, a software program that many readers will be aware of. Not so much now, maybe, but in years gone by, it came bundled with most new personal computer systems. It offered various entertainment options: from tuning into radio stations worldwide through to the playing of CDs. It was also possible to download music and save it to a hard disk.

I never download music to a computer. Unless you're under thirty or you're not serious about it, musical enjoyment becomes dependent upon the magical properties of the audio equipment. Consequently, although Apple has made a container load of cash from its 'iPods are cool' market, if you love music, it comes an extremely poor second to genuine hi-fi, as do computers. As you will surmise, I'm not a great fan of either cheap audio or cool gadgets. Occasionally, though, I did, when working (and with no quality music system in sight), listen to CDs on my laptop, and it was on such an occasion that I discovered 'the voice'.

As the Real Player One home page surfaced onto my screen, I noticed in the left-hand column there was a file by the name of 'Rick8'. I had never saved a file under that name or any file on Real Player One. Nonetheless, it immediately grabbed my attention, for, as I stated earlier, Rick was the name I was known as when a young boy. I certainly didn't use that name on the computer, and I don't speak to anyone via e-mail who would call me Rick. Hence, the whole thing struck me as odd.

The oddness factor climbed several notches when I played the Rick8 file. The TDC message left on Real Player says simply, "In Heaven." Then I decided to reverse it and heard, "we love you." Placing the two audio clips together, the message made more sense, *"In Heaven, we love you."*

Then there is the question, why Rick8? Why not Rick2, Rick5, Rick17, or just plain Rick? Was the number eight relevant? I've considered this problem at length and have managed to come up with only one suggestion. The figure-eight is universally believed to represent the joining of the two spheres of Heaven and Earth. Is it possible that the message was addressed to Rick and that the sender had left their address just in case there was any confusion as to where the voice had originated? A kind of heavenly postcode!

But had I had a direct message from Heaven? Surely, that is like someone saying, "Here you are, download this software application, and you can have the same experience as Moses." Yet, I can't find a reasonable alternative.

Holy, He is Author and Minister

"Sometimes you'll have the world telling you one thing, while your spirit guides are telling you something completely different. Who and what are you going to listen to?"

Scarlet Jei Saoirse

Throughout my life, I have had a companion – a 17th-century monk from the island of Sicily. I have never seen the monk. However, several other people have. The first time was in 1983 when an acquaintance, Marilyn, suddenly yelled out: "A monk is standing next to you!" She wasn't psychic or particularly sensitive to other realms, so this surprised her, and she slept with the light on for several nights following this incident. I have no idea why Marilyn saw the monk, and it was the first time I had heard of him.

He reappeared in 1992, according to a local psychic medium, who told me: "There's someone with you who looks like a monk; he goes way back and is some kind of guide. I can see him now standing at your shoulder."

Two years later, a close friend, Sylvia, saw the monk. I had made her a coffee and disappeared back into the kitchen. When I returned, she looked utterly traumatised, saying, "I've just seen a monk standing on your stairs looking right at me." There was a strong attraction between Sylvia and me, but in the end, the relationship collapsed. And I'm not sure if it was because of me or because of the monk.

The monk was seen in 2015 when a psychic medium, who I had never met before, sat down in my lounge and, within just two minutes of arriving, proclaimed, "There's a monk with you. I can see him standing just behind you. He doesn't have a hood, but he seems like a monk to me. He's very old." This medium, Pauline, has since become a friend and has mentioned the monk on several occasions.

The monk was then seen at a funeral in Lincolnshire in the summer of 2016. I had arrived at the crematorium alone; my wife was ill with man-flu. While waiting for the main party to arrive, I struck up a conversation with a lady named June. If I'm honest, I thought her a bit odd but nice. She was open, friendly, and chatty. In fact, within ten minutes of saying "hello," I discovered she was into crystals. Now, I'll confess that I'm not sure what to make of the whole crystal craze, but I'm not dismissive. I just listened politely and nodded in all the right places.

June and I, along with around thirty other mourners, were gathered outside the crematorium when the hearse pulled up. We were waiting for the casket to be carried into the chapel. Everything went silent. You could hear a pin drop when June leaned over and whispered to me, "There's a monk with you." I think I freaked her out a little by replying in hushed tones, "Yes, I know."

Utilising TDC, I have picked up numerous voices talking about 'the monk'. The first time was in 2004 when a friend and I discussed the possibility of guardian angels or guides. We were recording the conversation, and where I wondered, half-jokingly, who my guide was, an unmistakable voice came through that said, *"Holy, he is author and minister."*

Over the years, there have other voices that pointed to my priestly companion, but none as clear as the one heard in the summer of 2015, *"Remember you're a monk."* It was extraordinarily clear and seemed to claim that not only was my 'guide' a monk, but I was, too, in a former lifetime.

Help; Somebody Shot Me

"Maybe love at first sight isn't what we think it is. Maybe it's recognising a soul we loved in a past life and falling in love with them again."
Kamand Kojouri

Many think of reincarnation as an Eastern concept, and it does indeed originate in the world's oldest religion, Hinduism. However, it has thrived in the West for thousands of years; Pythagoras, Plato, and Plotinus are just three famous philosophers who accepted and taught reincarnation. Many readers may also be surprised to discover that the theory of reincarnation was prevalent amongst Christians during the first few centuries of Christianity. Not only the 'man on the street' type of Christian either; leading figures and 'Fathers' of the early Church supported and promoted the belief.

Saint Augustine (354-430 AD), for instance, once wrote: "The message of Plato, the purest and most luminous in all philosophy, has at last scattered the darkness of error, and now shines forth mainly to Plotinus, a Platonist so like his master that one would think they lived together, or rather – since so long a period of time separates them – that Plato is born again in Plotinus" *(Augustine, 'Contra Academicos')*.

My involvement with reincarnation began a couple of months after hearing the initial TDC from my father. The death of a parent serves as a reminder that we are all flesh and blood, existing in finite time. It can change your perspective on things. It also serves as a reminder that everyone suffers, worries, judges, and makes frequent errors. No one's life is really what it looks like on Facebook.

Cosmetic surgery will not change the fact that you will die. But exactly how many times do we die? That was the question that arose after I discovered another fascinating piece of TDC, and this time it explained my once intense interest in all things Jewish, "*You're a Jewish boy who is dead.*" Some years later, this Jewish connection was strengthened when a message concerning my stepdaughter came through via her mother, "*My Sarah, she was Jewish.*" Consequently, there does appear to be a Jewish thing going on in my soul group.

This type of voice needs a little explaining and will introduce another aspect of TDC. I have discovered over the years that, under certain circumstances, it is possible to communicate with the soul of a living person, with their day-to-day consciousness having no idea whatsoever that this is happening. In the case of "My Sarah, she was Jewish," it was a mother, my wife, talking about her daughter, whose middle name in this life is Sarah. Perhaps this was her name in the Jewish life, too; Sarah is a Jewish name.

Nowadays, many people think they have previously been a Native American Indian or a Chinese sage or Cleopatra or Queen Elizabeth I. It can get a little strange at times, with some New-Agers taking 'Come as You Were' reincarnation parties quite seriously. But the 'real' stuff, where could I find sensible research on reincarnation?

"Either Dr Stevenson is making a colossal mistake, or he will be known as the Galileo of the 20th-century" (Dr Harold Lief in the 'Journal of Nervous and Mental Disease' (Lief 1977).

By accumulating thousands of cases of children who spontaneously (without the need of hypnosis) recalled a past life, Dr Ian Stevenson provides persuasive scientific evidence, if not proof, for reincarnation.

In each case of past life memory, Stevenson methodically documents the child's statements. He then identifies the deceased person the child remembers being and verifies the facts of the dead person's life that match the child's memory. He even matches birthmarks and congenital disabilities to wounds and scars on the deceased, validated by medical records. His rigorous methods systematically remove all possible 'normal' explanations for the child's recollections.

Stevenson devoted the last forty years of his life to the scientific documentation of past life memories of children worldwide. He had over three thousand cases in his files. Many people, including sceptics and scholars, agree that these cases offer the best evidence for reincarnation.

Stevenson's credentials were impeccable. He was a medical doctor and had many scholarly papers to his credit before he began paranormal research. He was the head of the Department of Psychiatry at the University of Virginia and Director of the Division of Personality Studies at the same university.

Many people have not heard of Stevenson because he published primarily for the academic and scientific community. His writing – densely packed with research details and academic argument – is difficult for the average reader to follow. Moreover, he intentionally shunned the popular media to prevent reporters from sensationalising his research. He refused to appear on TV or radio, and he rarely granted magazine interviews.

An important researcher in the field of reincarnation, he compiled volumes of veridical evidence, matching memories with historical/census-type records, which in the cases of some children included accurate addresses.

This, in turn, led to reunions between these children and their still-living past-life parents.

Stevenson passed away on 8 February 2007, in Charlottesville, Virginia, at the age of eighty-eight. His work continues to impress me greatly, but a new piece of the jigsaw was put into place when a friend introduced me to a book entitled 'Beyond the Ashes' by Rabbi Yonassan Gershom. In this intriguing work, Rabbi Gershom presents research to support what many people think is a seemingly impossible phenomenon: the prospect that men and women living today perished in their past lives in the Holocaust.

Upon reading this book, which has become something of a classic in its field, I began to realise that what he was suggesting was a legitimate possibility. It is well written and well researched. The various ordinary people who had experienced Holocaust memories seemed not only genuine but also, at times, willing to do anything to protect their privacy. These people were not a crazy group of publicity seekers. Whatever was happening, it was an authentic experience for them.

As I continued to consider the possibility of a Jewish past life, I carried out several experiments, held conversations with friends about the subject, and searched for TDCs. I also had several dreams about a big city, which I was convinced was in Eastern Europe. Intuition told me it could be Budapest. Now intuition had led me up several ludicrous garden paths in the past, but it led straight into an intriguing mystery in this instance.

Budapest is quite rightly known throughout the world for its beauty and culture. Bustling but peaceful, a big yet friendly metropolis, it treasures the old and embraces the new. It is an architect's city. Walk one block, and several different schools of art assault you: the Parisian belle époque, High Austrian fin de siècle, Art Deco, some

Gothic, a little neo-Renaissance, Baroque and Hungary's very own Sezessionistil - facades full of allegorical friezes, arcades of caryatids and Zsolnay tiles, which is a kind of Magyar faience. I needed to visit this city.

Before setting off for Budapest, I described the city I saw to my wife, Diane; I had dreamt of it on several occasions. With a Masters Degree in psychotherapy, she is incredibly open-minded and didn't bat an eyelid as I explained about the one street in particular that returned again and again in my dreams. I described it in some detail.

On our first day in Budapest, we found it. Okay, it wasn't the same street; it was too short, but it was indicative of Budapest architecture, and 'my' street could be just around the corner – or ten miles away. Having said that, although I did feel very much at home in the city, there was no great sense of catharsis and no genuine leads for future investigation.

Yet, once back in the UK, I noticed a BIG change in my thought patterns and interests. Thoughts of the Holocaust no longer plagued me; my lifelong interest in Jewish culture melted away, and my mood lightened. Then just one week after returning from Budapest, I visited a friend in Yorkshire, a psychic lady named Jane, to let her hear TDC for the first time and carry out a discussion for further research.

As we were talking, she began to sense something around me. Describing a man with a cane (with badges somehow attached to it), she said, "I can just feel that behind you." The accompanying TDC noted, *"In the Republic City Park."*

I had been standing in City Park in Budapest just a few days earlier. The Republic of Hungary had made a big impression on me. It had certainly improved my mental health. However, the question is, did returning to the location of a past life somehow burst an 'emotional bubble', leaving me more at peace with both the past and the present? It's only a hypothesis, but with the aid of TDC, it has become a pretty good one.

I had always found it difficult to trust most people, and I worried about family and loved ones to an excessive degree. It was something deeply embedded in my psyche. So in executing the next TDC experiment, I was attempting to discover whether there was a link between this behaviour and a past life, perhaps in Hungary.

It did not take me long to uncover the answer. Asking whether there was anything from a past existence that had been affecting this life, I received an unequivocal response, *"Now seeing its influence."* Yet another spirit declared, *"This life has happened; now we feel it."* Therefore, it does appear - at least according to Spirit - that we carry over thoughts and emotional responses from former lives.

There was one other TDC that grabbed my attention.

Being ambushed is the same wherever it takes place, no matter who is involved. In a pub wearing jeans or in a jungle clothed in camouflage, it is the same thing. I had been ambushed and hospitalised in the past and had become very 'streetwise'. While talking about this, I received the following message, *"Help; somebody shot me."* In this instance, therefore, I was listening to the voice of my own soul, in a similar way to listening to my wife talking about Sarah.

I had had dreams of being shot, too, after being ambushed up a blind alley by soldiers. I was shot in the left side of my stomach. I am precise about where I was shot in the dream because I have had health issues in that area, including a recurring ulcer. If we are to believe Dr Stevenson - and I encourage those who find themselves interested to obtain a copy of his book 'Biology &

Reincarnation' - this may well be the effect of trauma in a previous life.

This is significant. It helps us to compile a 'map' of the territory that we are investigating. We are always searching for clues and possibilities, so it is imperative to dissect the meaning of various TDC statements continually. Was I Jewish in a past life? Was I shot, perhaps by soldiers, in Budapest? I don't know, but the 'flags' are there. Taking it at face value, it would appear that although this was not the life that is most affecting my current incarnation – we will come to this soon – it was having some effect on it. Furthermore, it suggested that it is not necessarily the 'next life' where karmic debts are paid, as we shall see. There can be a considerable gap before the balance due is called in.

Look for the Vineyard

"You may have the universe if I may have Italy."
Giuseppe Verdi

Pauline, the psychic medium, did not only tell me that there was a monk with me; one evening, she turned up on my doorstep with a few scribbled notes, quite literally on the back of an envelope. They had come to her in a kind of trance state in the middle of the night, and she had written them down quickly, the first word being 'winter'. "Do they mean anything to you?" she asked. "They are something to do with your monk."

In addition to 'winter', several other words and names were jotted down – Pedara, Pallaro, Borg, Santo, St. Paulinus, Pachino, Antonio, Catherine, Vivaldi, and Winged Lion. Finally, a message, 'look for the vineyard'. A bit of a hotchpotch really; not even a decent Scrabble score.

And so it was that I began to research the various bits of information that Pauline had given me, starting with the three Ps: Pedara, Pallaro, and Pachino.

I first looked up Pedara and found it to be a commune (municipality) in the Province of Catania on the Italian island of Sicily. It was also, I discovered, a village within 'the vineyards of Catania' a few hundred years ago.

I then looked up Pallaro, but that drew a bit of a blank; it was merely an Italian surname (at least I thought so at this time). All the same, there was an Italian theme surfacing, and if Pachino turned out to have something to do with Italy, I thought I might be on to something. Pachino, it turned out, was indeed Italian. It was a town and commune in the Province of Siracusa, Sicily: south-eastern Sicily, to be more exact, not a million miles from Catania.

Archimedes had his eureka moment in a bath in Siracusa, and I was soon to have one of my own. What made this discovery even more impressive was that the name 'Pachino' derives from the Latin word 'Bacchus', the Greek and Roman god of wine, and the word vinum, which means wine in Latin. South-east Sicily is wine-growing country, and my mind once again went to Pauline's scrawled message on the back of an envelope – 'look for the vineyard'.

It was like someone or something had channelled a message through Pauline that was pointing me in the direction of Sicily. I moved onto Antonio and Catherine; did these two names have any connection with Sicily? By now, I was not too surprised to discover that they did. They were linked to Pedaro – the Basilica of St. Catherine and the Church of St. Antonio could be found in the town.

Next up was St. Paulinus – more precisely, St Paulinus of Nola, a friend and contemporary of St. Augustine. He was originally from Bordeaux in France, where he was born to a high-ranking family, receiving an exceptional literary education, his teacher being the poet Ausonius. However, St. Paulinus was to sell all of his assets for the benefit of the poor and was ordained as a priest in Barcelona. He became the successor to the chair of Nola, near Naples, after the death of its bishop around 409. His bones can now found in the small Sicilian city of Sutera, about 43 miles southeast of Palermo, Sicily, where they dedicate a feast day and conduct a procession for the saint at Easter each year.

Santo, of course, was easily explained; it is simply the Italian word for 'saint'. But what of Borg? My first thought was that the Borg was one of the deadliest, most ruthless sci-fi villains ever created, as all fans of the TV show Star Trek will know. Then there was Marcus Borg, the internationally revered 'Jesus scholar', who passed away in January 2015. This seemed much more likely, and initially, I followed this path of exploration. It proved to be a dead-end. This part of my search proved to be the most frustrating of all. But I've always believed that frustration can be an elevator – a way to reach a new level quickly.

I still couldn't track down anything relevant to do with Vivaldi or the Winged Lion either, and Borg continued to be something of a mystery, too. I would need to keep searching if I was to make any sense of these.

Nevertheless, within days of discovering the Sicily connection, my wife, Diane, and I had booked airline tickets to Catania for April 2017. I needed a few months in-between to work out exactly where we were going to visit and what we were looking for. Sicily is a big island, and we only had a week due to work commitments. As a result, we booked four nights at a beach villa on the east coast near Pachino and three nights at a hotel in Pedara. Naturally, we hired a car, too; there would be a lot of miles to cover.

So what exactly was I aiming to find out when I arrived in Sicily?

First, I guess, would I feel any recognition? It had been suggested during a TDC session that I was a monk in a previous life. Could this have been in Sicily, more specifically, in the south-eastern corner of Sicily? Intuitively, I felt that this was a big part of the puzzle. However, I wasn't jumping to any conclusions. My intuition is usually excellent, but I was more than aware that it could lead me astray on occasion. I needed to keep my feet on the floor. I didn't want any self-fulfilling prophecies.

Secondly, I was perhaps looking for some enlightenment concerning my current life. Why would a long 'dead' monk direct me to the island of Sicily if not for enlightenment about something or other? It could not, I reasoned, be simply to let me catch a glimpse of a past life. I could have been told about that back home. This appeared to be more urgent, perhaps even to do with my health.

In his study entitled 'Birth Marks and Birth Defects Corresponding to Wounds on Deceased Persons', Dr Stevenson outlined a link between the concept of reincarnation, birthmarks and congenital disabilities. 'The congenital disabilities were nearly always of rare types. In cases in which a deceased person was identified, the details of whose life unmistakably matched the child's statements, a close correspondence was nearly always found between the birthmarks and/or congenital disabilities on the child and those found on the deceased person,' he wrote.

As we will see shortly, my death in the Sicilian past life was brought about by asphyxiation. This condition arises from a deficient supply of oxygen to the body, causing abnormal breathing, resulting in unconsciousness and often death. I suffer from obstructive sleep apnoea in this life, a disorder in which breathing is briefly and repeatedly interrupted during sleep. It occurs when the muscles in the back of the throat fail to keep the airway open, despite efforts to breathe, causing disturbed sleep and oxygen starvation.

I was diagnosed with sleep apnoea in 2018, although I had probably been battling it for several years before. However, this was not the first time I had been affected by the inability to breathe, resulting in a deficient oxygen supply to the body. In March 1970 (I can't recall the exact date, but I wouldn't be surprised if it was the day I died in

Sicily), I awoke to gasp for breath. I was just thirteen years of age at the time, and horrified, my parents suddenly heard me crying out, "oxygen, oxygen." The doctor was called, but no diagnosis was given, simply being passed off as 'one of those things', which of course, in many ways, it was. Nevertheless, I now believe that there was a cause, particularly after developing sleep apnoea in later life. A TDC supports this belief, stating, *"The air from the northern slopes got him."*

Further research strongly suggested that I lived my life as a monk primarily at the Convent of the Capuchin Fathers, located on the northern slopes of Mount Etna.

After several dreams in which I was in the presence of monks all wearing beards, I discovered that all Capuchin fathers had facial hair. It was a tradition. I have had facial hair ever since I could grow it. Naturally, that could be just another coincidence, but it is another pointer, as were the TDC voices that came out of the speakers of my computer, *"You are a Capuchin"* and *"With the Capuchins."*

Look, the Mountain

"Listen and attend with the ear of your heart."
Saint Benedict of Nursia

Sicily is at the crossroads of the Mediterranean, with every neighbouring power having occupied the island, including the Greeks, Arabs, and Normans. Its incredible diversity of landscapes, the pervasive scent of lemon trees, the purity of early morning light, and the sight of Mount Etna erupting against an evening sky continues to entice visitors today. It's no surprise that the locals refer to it as the Garden of Eden.

My visit had a different purpose than to enjoy the sights, sounds, and aromas of this fascinating island, although that purpose was somewhat tricky to understand. I was indeed frustrated with my life in England. I had become so tired of keeping up with Mr and Mrs Jones, of being constantly bombarded by advertising, of having brands pushed in my face at every turn. I had become sick of lying politicians and greedy business people, was done entirely with what the 21st-century calls entertainment, where everything is so dumbed-down, and I had had enough of rude, thoughtless people. And it had exhausted me; I was in a constant state of fatigue. Yet, I still wasn't sure of the reason I was being led to Sicily.

Then a new lead came from a source very close by, my eldest stepdaughter, Mandy. An intelligent, very spiritually aware woman in her early 30s, Mandy had shown interest in the trip to Sicily. At one stage, I suggested that she should maybe come with us. The response surprised me, with Mandy explaining that she had had nightmares of being killed in a volcanic eruption since she was a child and had no wish to visit an island with the most active volcano in Europe.

This started me thinking. I was told to 'look for the vineyard', and Mandy is a professional wine grower. Could she have had a life in Sicily, too? I had known her for 15 years, and I've always felt close to her for reasons I couldn't quite pin down. Yes, she had always been a pleasure to be around, but there was something more profound at a spiritual level. Maybe this was it.

This was underlined when I discovered a TDC stating, *"Seventh of March is not nothing for you and Mandy."* In 1669, Mount Etna erupted on 8 March.

Another 'meaningless coincidence' occurred when I homed in on 1669, the year that Etna rained terror on the surrounding countryside and the city of Catania. Almost immediately, I found the monastery of St Nicola l'Arena located just a couple of miles away from Pedara. It was, I discovered, a monastery with a vineyard. Was this the vineyard I was looking for? Most of the monks had left by 1669, moving to a new monastery in Catania because of the risk of Etna erupting. Although a few monks were left behind to tend the grapes and other crops, this proved to be the right decision.

So, at this stage, we had a year, a monastery (which turned out to be Benedictine), and the vineyard, the latter two within a couple of miles of one of the towns I was being sent to. Nicolosi, the town in question and home of the St Nicola l'Arena monastery, was also known as Nicolosi-Pedara.

I was delighted to find out that the monastery, now mostly in ruins, is home to a museum and a local authority. I would be able to visit it. A few days before flying to Sicily, I had dreamt of standing on top of a building with medieval castle battlements. It was covered in snow, with giant snowballs (a couple of feet in diameter) lined up along the one wall. As I looked out, there was also a large tree perhaps fifty yards from the wall. I instinctively knew this was something to do with the Sicilian past life. Nicolosi, I discovered, is a ski centre, so even the weather pattern began to fit into the overall picture.

But there was more. In 1993, I began to utilise an old desk diary for comments on various paranormal matters, including gematria (a system by which hidden truths and meanings are discovered within words), which I was very interested in at the time. Most of the book's pages contain scribblings, many of which have entirely lost their meaning as I can't remember why I wrote them down in the first place. Nevertheless, on the one page, I found two years that I recall being given in a half-sleep state -1669 and 1444. Now, 1669 I had already found but was having little luck with 1444.

However, early in March 2017, Etna blew, and my wife informed me straight away as she is a former geologist with a particular interest in volcanoes. As a result, I found myself Googling the event and entirely by accident found a page that stated the following: 'The village of Nicolosi, founded by Benedictine monks in 1437, was wiped out by an eruption in 1669. In 1444 there was another great eruption on Nicolosi; an eruption of great moment since it threatened Catania'. The article also stated that the cone fell into the crater and that a tremendous earthquake accompanied the eruption.

After learning about the 1669 eruption and Mandy's 'volcano phobia,' I joked with her that it would be okay to come to Sicily since the nightmare of asphyxiation (the kind of death she remembers) because of an erupting volcano is not going to happen to anyone twice. When I found the reference to 1444, though, I was no longer quite so sure.

It was around this time that I also began to receive other voices via TDC. One was incredibly enigmatic, stating, *"Look for your brother. If you find him, he will not lie to you."* I had no idea what this meant. Surely, I was not looking for a living, breathing person. Or maybe I was. Perhaps I was seeking a place where I could find the remains of someone. I just didn't know.

But it was underlined to me that this region of Sicily was formerly my home, with messages such as *"You were alive on Mount Etna," "You climbed Etna,"* and *"Look, the mountain."*

Further research allowed me to find answers for the 'Winged Lion' and 'Vivaldi' conundrums. The Winged Lion, I knew, was the heraldic symbol of Mark the Evangelist; what I hadn't realised is that it is also a symbol for 'peace'. The Benedictine motto is 'Pax', which is Latin for 'Peace'. We were being led, it seemed, to a Benedictine monastery.

As for Vivaldi, that had me stumped. I knew that he was a Baroque composer born in Venice whose most famous work is The Four Seasons. I also knew that he was born on 4 March 1678. It was my love of music that helped me to solve this final puzzle. I was searching for information on one of Vivaldi's compositions, his Laudate pueri Dominum (RV 601), when I stumbled on what was, for me, a staggering piece of information. Until 1962, when his birth registration was found, he was for over three hundred years believed to have been born in 1669!

The universe was underlining all of the information it was giving me, often in imaginative ways that were linked to my own interests, in this instance, music.

It was time to get on that plane.

Ancient Fishing Village

"People fish because they are searching for something.
Often it is not for a fish."
Fennel Hudson, Fly Fishing - Fennel's Journal - No. 5

I was going in blind, arriving in Sicily with several pieces of information from a psychic, some TDC messages, details of a few dreams ... and the monk.

When we arrived in Sicily, the first port of call was a village named Portopalo, on the island's south-eastern corner. A few miles from Pachino, it was straddled between the Ionian and Mediterranean Seas, a small town of about twenty-two-thousand inhabitants. It is the home of Nero d'Avola wine and very possibly the finest cherry tomatoes in the world. It is a tight grid of narrow one-way streets that centres on a broad piazza. It's a Piet Mondrian painting in urban form.

Knowing that we had been led to Pachino, we looked around the main square in anticipation as we tucked into our first breakfast. I don't know what we were expecting to see: the appearance of a ghostly monk walking in front of the church? Recognition of something long forgotten? In any event, we didn't see or recognise anything. But we were not too concerned, as I was sure that the instruction to visit this town more than likely referred to the coastal fishing village of Marzamemi. This was said to be the original Pachino, as the town we know today was not established until several decades after 1669.

Marzamemi is one of Sicily's prettiest seaside villages. The Arabs in the 10th-century named the village, which translates as something along the lines of Turtle Dove Bay. They also built the original tonnara (tuna processing plant), which became one the most important on the island. Although the tonnara is no longer functioning, Marzamemi still plays host to various fishing and processing activities.

Its wonderfully balmy alfresco atmosphere invites you to sit back, relax, and enjoy a glass of prosecco and some antipasti, which is what we did. We stayed in Marzamemi for a little over three hours, at one stage enjoying Sicilian cheesecake (cheesecake will never be the same again) and another glass of prosecco.

As we were leaving Marzamemi, we rested on a low wall; I think Diane wanted to stop and tie a shoelace or some other such mundane thing. It turned out to be quite an auspicious moment, though. Diane turned to me and said: "Have you seen that sign?" She looked vaguely shocked, as did I when I looked up onto the side of an old building and read the words 'Antico Borgo dei Pesca' – or 'Ancient Fishing Village'.

It was 'Borg' with an additional letter, the Italian word for village. I was sent to Pachino, but the real destination was the ancient fishing village of Marzamemi, or the antico borgo dei pesca. I had figured this might be the case before we even left Britain, but this underlined it most dramatically. At this time, I started to believe wholeheartedly that this was where I was from in a past life. And further evidence was to come several hours later once back at the villa.

It was just getting dark when I received a call from Booking.com to inform me that the hotel I had booked in Pedara had had an 'occurrence' and was no longer available. I was standing on the roof terrace when I received the call, looking north up the coast towards our next destination. The guy on the phone said to me: "We have managed to find you other accommodation ... in Nicolosi."

Nicolosi, as already mentioned, is just a couple of miles away from Pedara. It is also the village where the monastery sits, something I didn't know when I made the reservations. The strangeness factor continued to rise, yet the feeling was so dewdrop delicate that one couldn't grasp it any more than one could catch a bubble.

Stop!

"Pay attention to your life, and you will see bits of 'magic' that happen precisely when you need them to happen."
Linda Westphal

Arriving in Nicolosi, we found our B&B quite quickly, in the heart of the village and the shadow of Mount Etna. For the equivalent of around £80 a night, we had a delightful bedroom with a balcony, a lovely bathroom, and even our own kitchen. There was also a decorative 'door' at the top of one of the walls in the bedroom. The building used to house animals downstairs, and the 'loft' behind the door was used for keeping feedstuffs ... it was known as a 'pallaro'.

With one more piece of the jigsaw in place, we found ourselves walking up towards the monastery, about two miles away on the edge of the village. There was no problem in finding it; I just 'knew' where it was. I didn't have to ask or buy a map. What I didn't know was that on the day of our arrival, the grounds were closed. It was Sunday. It would be two days until we could gain entry and walk around the old monastery.

After a wonderful breakfast prepared, cooked, and served by our landlady, including muffins, eggs, cheeses, pastries, fruit, coffee, cakes, biscuits, rolls, yoghurt, cereals, and other delicacies, we decided to use Monday to visit Mount Etna, something that, being a geologist, Diane was particularly looking forward to. Unlike her daughter, she couldn't wait to peer down those vents!

Broom trees with their yellow, jasmine-scented blossoms line the road up from Nicolosi, followed by woodland and small shepherd refuges. Vineyards follow, then everything goes black and lava craters dot the landscape. We eventually arrived at the car park for the funicular railway, which carried intrepid adventurers up onto Etna. Diane was one of those adventurers - I stayed behind in the car; I'd been up the 'Beautiful Mountain', as the locals call it, before, and anyway, I wasn't feeling too good. I was exhausted.

I did stroll around a dozen souvenir shops (all of them selling precisely the same things) and stared open-mouthed at the glorious views along the coast and across the villages. I felt tired and nauseous and realised that, through overwork, this is how I felt back home all the time. It was like someone yelling 'stop!' That night, I had a dream with someone saying to me, "This is where we always brought the sick monks."

A Gift from Beyond the Veil

"Don't keep forever on the public road, going only where others have gone."
Alexander Graham Bell

My mind was racing – I would finally get to visit the monastery and walk around the grounds. It felt strange. I had always 'known' the medieval castle battlements would be there, but now I started to doubt it. It all seemed too good to be true, despite all of the instructions and psychic signposts. And if the medieval castle battlements were there, how would I feel? Would I receive any insights? What on earth was I doing here?

Sicily is awash with monasteries, churches, and other sacred places, and most of them are more visited than the monastery at Nicolosi. In fact, on the day we were there, we were on our own; no one else arrived during the entire two hours of our visit. This made it even more breathtaking.

The monastery of San Nicolo l'Arena derives from the 12th-century and, erected on a former chapel, was founded by Benedictine monks as a resting place for travellers and, I discovered, a hospice for the sick monks from nearby monasteries. It was built at the behest of Frederick II of Aragon, with the nearby village, Nicolosi, growing up around it and taking its name. The complex includes the church, crypt, and residential buildings.

As I walked through the main entrance to the monastery, an eight-hundred-year-old arch, it was still as the night apart from the sound of birdsong and the occasional bark of a distant dog.

This distinctive entrance was at the beginning of a beautiful path, with walls made of lava stone. The track was straight as a die for perhaps one hundred and fifty yards, where there was another arch in front of a yard where a 'four-mouth' tank is situated, a system of wells for drawing water for the monastery. The walk down the path felt so familiar and was identical to the path in my dreams, as were the arches. However, the structure on which the four-mouth tank was built took my breath away; it was a low construction, reached by climbing just half a dozen steps, but it had been designed in the manner of a castle, including medieval castle battlements.

I felt a shudder run down my spine. I knew this place. The sight bewildered me. Here, in the middle of a modern first-world country, I remembered a life that took place over three hundred years ago.

As I climbed the steps, I saw the tree I had dreamed of, correctly placed around fifty yards from the walls. Of course, this couldn't have been there three centuries ago, but maybe a similar tree was? I didn't know; all I could feel was a sense of peace mixed with slight trepidation. I felt as if I had had a love/hate relationship with this place. There was the calm and tranquillity, a sense of holiness, yet also a feeling of the devastation that occurred during the volcanic eruption of 1669. And there was the winter, the snow. What was that about? Could it still have been snowing as late in the year as 8 March, nearly three hundred and fifty years ago? I can't find any mention of that, so I assume not – it is, I believe, one of those things that would be written about in historical accounts if true. The other option is that winter was foretelling future troubles, which we will discuss in due course.

Diane and I stood on the structure for around fifteen minutes. Neither of us spoke. I didn't know the whole history of this place or why I was there. But for a short period, I felt 'out of time'. I sensed the despair, the sadness, the hopelessness of what had happened in and around Nicolosi, and I wanted to help but didn't know how. I guess I wanted to tell those long-dead monks and other workers employed at the monastery that they were not alone. That somebody still felt their suffering. Someone who was there to show he cares, about them, for who they were.

Diane could also feel the psychic energy of this magical location, and I was pretty sure she was at the heart of the story too. I had tracked down the connection with her daughter, and upon returning to the UK and asking questions about my wife's involvement back in 17th- century Sicily, I received the following TDC messages, *"Oh Roderick, your hearts connect"* and *"She is beautiful."* And one of the most impressive voices I picked up, simply because of the context in which it was recorded, simply said, *"Diane."* I had left the recording equipment running (by mistake) while I went outside to fetch something from my car. This voice, therefore, came out of total silence, and it is but a whisper but left me in no doubt that my wife was at the heart of the Sicilian story.

Sitting down on one of the 'four mouths', I saw an old badge lying alongside me, rusty and battered, with the solitary word 'Destinazion', which seemed to sum everything up at that particular moment in time. I slipped it into my pocket alongside a small piece of black lava from the structure's walls.

Continuing our tour of the monastery complex, we walked around the back of the main building. It was littered with all manner of buildings that the monks had previously utilised. These included cells, chapels, storerooms, a crypt; it was all here but now overgrown and in ruins. Then we walked through another arch and turned a corner, and there it was - the vineyard!

I walked towards it with my heart fluttering and the sensation of a million butterflies in my stomach. I had a feeling of complete recognition. I felt a sense of excitement, joy, contentment, and light-headedness. I will never forget seeing that vineyard (again!) for the first time in this life.

It was impossible to enter the vineyard as metal fences surrounded it. I recall staring up a path that went straight through the vineyard at a slight incline and into a forest beyond. I turned to Diane and said: "I want to go up that path!" Unfortunately, that was not possible, but when we returned home and showed Mandy the photos, she blurted out, "I want to go up that path!" as soon as she saw it. She remembered, too.

I went back to the B&B that evening, but my heart stayed behind. My encounter with the past taught me something. That in the face of the exhaustion I found myself in back in the UK, there was an answer – an answer of care, an answer of love. The monk had brought me 'home'.

My monk has certainly made contact with me regularly and, on one extraordinary occasion, stated, "Listen to the song," followed by the sound of monks chanting. This felt almost like a minor miracle, a gift from beyond the veil.

There is, of course, still much to learn from my trip to Sicily. I feel I have only touched the surface, and that eternal crossroads of the Mediterranean continues to call me back. There is still much to discover. But I now know that the TDC voice that said to me, *"Remember you're a monk"*, was stating a fact and has put me on a path that will last the rest of my life.

Where's the Crypt?

"The most beautiful act of faith is the one made in darkness, in sacrifice, and with extreme effort."
  Padre Pio

On a few occasions, events revolving around Christianity have had to be filed away into a draw I call 'strange and weird happenings'.

The Faces were a 70s rock n' roll band; their affable, back-to-basics (and frequently liquor-laden) concerts were events not to be missed, and my little 'gang' were committed to getting tickets. Consequently, along with several hundred fans in tartan scarves, several of my music-mad friends and I decided to queue all night outside of Birmingham Odeon for a show that was to take place a couple of months later.

In all, we would be queuing for something like fourteen hours; no sleeping bags, no flasks of coffee, no sense. We didn't care, though, mainly because we knew there was a Wimpy Bar just a couple of hundred yards up New Street that stayed open all night. Therefore, we took turns to walk up, grab a burger and a cola, sit down for thirty minutes and get warm.

Now I'm not even sure that Wimpy Bars still exist, so if you have no idea what a Wimpy Bar is, all I need to say is that it was a forerunner to McDonald's, a fast-food joint with lots of bright colours and plenty of plastic.

It was going on for two o'clock in the morning when two friends, Jack and Tony, and I decided to get some refreshment. We left three or four of our other mates in the queue to keep our places. We were all in high spirits when we reached the Wimpy Bar, even more so when an attractive young lady came and took our order. Yes, in those days, fast-food joints had waitresses, whereas today we've 'progressed' to a situation where we stand in line for fifteen minutes to be served food in fifteen seconds that was cooked an hour ago. But to perfectly honest, it didn't taste much better back then.

I can't recall what we had to eat and drink, but we had been there for more or less twenty minutes when a tall, well-built, and smartly dressed gentleman walked into the café, straight up to our table, and asked: "Can I join you?" We all looked around at the numerous empty tables and then back at each other in astonishment. Even so, we had been raised to be polite, so we signalled for him to sit down.

The first thing I noticed was that this man had a big head. I don't mean he was boastful or arrogant; he had what I considered to be a large, square head, with reasonably short brown hair and bright blue eyes. He was clean-shaven and, with a suit that appeared to have come straight out of Savile Row that very evening, looked like a very successful businessman.

"Where is the crypt?" was the very first thing he said to us.

Now this seemingly crazy question sparked a flurry of insults from my two compatriots; one, in particular, we shall say, Jack, was quite abusive. I felt embarrassed "Where are all the people; where is the crypt?" he asked again. Tony laughed like a hyena while Jack came out with a series of expletives. I sat there like a mute, a faint smile playing around my lips so as not to seem a killjoy, but feeling very awkward.

"Why do you talk to me this way," was all our new friend would say. He stayed totally calm, which I remember thinking was downright odd. I'd have thumped Jack ages ago!

I tried to change the direction this rather pointless conversation was going in. I noticed he had a giant cassette player with him and, being very interested in music, asked what he was listening to? "The Canterbury Cathedral Choir," he said as he pressed the 'on' button, "I was there earlier today." Now, although in those days, my musical tastes were more rock n' roll, I was immediately struck by the sacred music coming out of the speakers. Even back then, religion was not alien to me. I prayed at night, a little confessional of my own, and I had always enjoyed sacred music, whether it be Christmas Carols or thumping anthems such as Jerusalem. Jack was less impressed. "What the hell's that, you moron?" The 'man' just looked at Jack, not in anger, or even in pity, just 'looked'. I could feel Jack start to become unnerved, although unfortunately, this made him even more abusive. If truth be told, there was a right old noise coming from our table, and soon the waitress arrived asking us to tone it down and telling us to switch off the music. The man smiled and pressed the 'off' button straightaway. He also informed the waitress that he would not require any food or drink.

It was a strange atmosphere, and once again, the question was asked: "Where is the crypt?" In those days, I didn't even know what a crypt was besides being 'under' a church', my best guess being a cellar where they kept the communion wine and a couple of long-dead corpses. I have since learned that crypts house the bodies of saints under the High Altar. On this particular autumn evening, though, I didn't understand what a crypt was. So I asked.

The man didn't reply.

I tried another question. "Where are you staying?"

"I'm just passing through," he replied calmly.

It was past two in the morning! Surely, he was staying somewhere in the city. And what was a businessman with a tape recorder doing in a Wimpy Bar at that time of the morning anyway, apart from trying to find out where the crypt was?

"What do you do for a living?" I tried once again to elicit some information.

"I'm a traveller," was the enigmatic reply.

Even I was starting to feel exasperated. Once again, Jack began to throw insults left, right, and centre. And fair play to his insanity, he was doing this without having had any alcoholic beverage at all (and the most potent drugs any of us ever took were aspirin). Not knowing where to put myself, I looked down at the table and caught sight of the man's hands and, because his jacket cuffs had risen, his wrists. The first thing I noticed was what looked like an astonishingly expensive gold wristwatch. Was it a Rolex? I don't know. In reality, I don't think I knew what a Rolex was in those days. But it cost a few bob, that much was certain. It wasn't the watch that kept my gaze glued to his wrists, though.

The man sitting opposite me had stigmata marks. A dictionary would probably describe these as bodily marks or sores in locations corresponding to the crucifixion wounds of Jesus, such as the hands and feet. Of course, despite all of the religious imagery, archaeological evidence has now proven that the nails were driven through the wrists, not the hands. And this guy had the stigmata marks in precisely the right place. There was around half an inch of circular scabbing on both wrists and, I soon discovered, on both sides, so four scabs in all.

I continued to stare for what must have been twenty or thirty seconds before I felt Jack dig me in the ribs and shout: "Come on, let's get back to the crypt!"

We all rose, including the man, and as I was about to walk out, I looked at him and said cheerily: "See you then," in a manner I used with everyone. I will never forget what happened next. He seemed to look straight into my soul with his piercing blue eyes and responded gently: "Yes ... you will."

With that, he turned and walked towards the door. We were a few steps behind him. Anyone who knows New Street in Birmingham will realise that it is a long, wide, and straight thoroughfare. Nowadays, it is pedestrianised; back then, it wasn't. Apart from that, it's more or less the same. It's not an easy place to disappear from sight in the early hours. But that's what the man looking for the crypt did. We could have been no more than five seconds behind him, yet he'd vanished when we got outside. Unless he was hiding in a doorway, it was hard to see how?

I do have a possible answer, though. Utilising TDC, I asked my spirit friends if they could tell me anything about the man in the Wimpy Bar. The answer was fascinating, taking in eight separate statements, all back-to-back, over just one solitary minute: *"He was not really there ... he was back in the Capuchin monastery ... you have now an answer with the monk ... it happened when the timing was right ... I've got seconds before I leave, Roderick ... you look whacked out ... you are in love ... Diane."*

The answer incorporated more than I asked for, but perhaps the most interesting claim was that the man in the Wimpy Bar was not actually there; he was back in the Capuchin monastery!

This explanation smacks of bilocation, which several saints have achieved, including Saint Martin de Porres of Lima, Peru. Very reliable eyewitnesses testified that Saint Martin de Porres was seen doing missionary work in Asia and Mexico, even though he never left Lima.

Padre Pio, an Italian priest who became celebrated worldwide for his psychic gifts, is perhaps the most famous person to bilocate. Even though he hardly ever left the village, San Giovanni Rotondo, where he worked in the local church, witnesses reported seeing him in other places all over the world.

He spent many hours praying and meditating and once said of meditation: "Through the study of books, one sees God; by meditation, one finds him." His deep love for prayer and meditation may have contributed to his ability to bilocate. It has been suggested that the thought energy expressed while praying or meditating intensely may manifest in physical ways across time and space.

The most well-known of the countless different bilocation stories about Padre Pio comes from World War II. During war bombing raids over Italy in 1943 and 1944, Allied aircraft from several different missions returned to their bases without dropping their bombs. The reason, they reported, was that a man identical to Padre Pio's description appeared in the air outside of their aircraft, right in front of their guns. The bearded priest waved his hands and arms frantically, indicating that they must stop, while looking at them with eyes that seemed to be lit with flames of fire. American and British pilots and crew members from various squadrons swapped stories about their experiences with Padre Pio. He had bilocated to try to protect his village from being destroyed. No bombs were ever dropped on that area during World War II.

Padre Pio is also one of the few saints who have suffered Christ's Passion's wounds, the stigmata. In addition to the wounds of the nails and the spear, he was also given the laceration that Christ endured on his shoulder, an injury caused by carrying the cross. However, I am not claiming that the man in the Wimpy Bar was Padre Pio, even though he was a Capuchin. If my memory serves me correctly, he didn't look like Padre Pio. My guy was another Capuchin with the stigmata who could bilocate. That has to be a small club, surely?

I will share just one more 'mystical' event linked to Christianity, an experience concerning a holy man – St. Jerome, a priest, confessor, theologian, and historian. He also became a Doctor of the Church. Today, he is recognised as a saint by the Roman Catholic Church, the Eastern Orthodox Church, the Lutheran Church, and the Church of England. In the annals of Christianity, he is a big hitter. He was also highly outspoken, which is why I came across him.

Almost all Christian scholars nowadays believe that Mark's was the first Gospel ever written. However, tradition has it that Matthew was the first, hence being placed first in the New Testament. I had been doing a little research and had concluded that there was a genuine possibility that Matthew's was indeed the first Gospel to be written, although the version we have today has been added to and edited. This is not the place to go into details, but I believed my reasoning was sound. However, the people who disagreed with me comprised some of the finest minds of the modern age.

Then I had a very unusual dream. I found myself talking to St. Jerome. How I knew it was St. Jerome, I don't know, as I knew nothing at all about him. I'd heard the name, but that was a far as it went.

I couldn't make out what was said, and the surroundings were completely white; it was like being in an enormous white box. Then St. Jerome introduced me to someone else. I wasn't given a name in the dream, but I did see that he was blind and had a filthy rag wrapped around his eyes. It was a compelling dream, and so once awake, I began to do a little research.

I discovered that St. Jerome not only claimed to have seen a Hebrew gospel, but he had also translated it and, on several occasions, had quoted from it. It is generally accepted that the 'Gospel according to the Hebrews' existed and was called 'Matthew' by some of its users. Various writers in the early Church quoted short passages from it, and scholars have identified over fifty such fragments. A much earlier writer than Jerome, Papias, a disciple of John, the apostle, stated that Matthew recorded the sayings of Jesus in Hebrew. Everyone then translated them as best he could. It is unlikely that the book to which Papias refers is the New Testament Gospel of Matthew. It is quite possible, though, that Papias' 'Matthew' is the same as Jerome's Hebrew gospel. In other words, it was the original gospel of Matthew before 'everyone translated it as best they could'. One of those translations became the gospel of Matthew we know today.

There was still more, though. I found out that around 373 AD, St. Jerome travelled to Alexandria in Egypt to hear someone extraordinary talk about the Holy Spirit and Christianity in general. His name was Didymus the Blind, and he too believed that Matthew's was the first Gospel.

By now, you will not be surprised to discover that I have also received numerous TDC messages underlining my Christian heritage in a spiritual sense. These include: *"You have served the shepherd", "You are still serving the shepherd",* and *"Rod, you have served the fisherman."* On one occasion, I was recording a conversation with my soon to be wife, which picked up our souls talking to each other (unknown to our everyday consciousness, which was in this instance discussing family problems), saying, *"I think I love you (wife) ... I serve the shepherd (me)."*

I also recall visiting India in 2008, a wonderful country. What's more, like many people, I travelled expecting to find a deep spirituality. Yet, despite the magnificent temples and the apparent faith of most people, I felt nothing. I only began to understand why when I returned to the UK and received the message, *"India, the problem is you're Christian."* So these Christian motifs do tend to float around me.

Nothing Would be the Same Again

"Theologians may quarrel, but the mystics of the world speak the same language."
Meister Eckhart

My early adolescence through mid-twenties was a whirlwind of activity. I worked for a short time on the Spanish island of Mallorca and the Italian Adriatic coast. I walked away from the vast majority of my friends for good when I was twenty-five because I knew that I would never fulfil whatever potential I might have if I continued doing the same things day after day. I think I sensed that the only way I would beat those kids was to wiggle out of my position.

I then went into business with an old friend. I needed to immerse myself in something new. For a short time, I became very materialistic. We were dealing with oil companies and commodities – greed was rife. I did become a vegetarian at this time, a philosophy I have continued to follow for the past thirty-nine years. But this was the only positive to come out of this period until something happened that changed my entire outlook on everything.

I had known my business partner's wife, Catherine, since schooldays, and it was with Catherine that I enjoyed the most amazing spiritual experience of my entire life.

Mystical experiences aren't something taught about in schools or discussed very much in society. When they are discussed, they are often misunderstood, or even worse, assumed to signify a kind of madness. Moreover, they often defy physical description, incorporating a total absorption into something so huge and so 'other' that words can't suffice.

Despite that, I shall attempt to describe my experience as best I can. It happened in the early hours of 26 January 1983, in a quiet suburb of England's second city, Birmingham. It lasted for eight hours, from 1.00 am until 9.00 am and changed my life forever.

Catherine and I had a mutual interest in 'things that go bump in the night', and one evening after her husband had gone to bed, we sat down with a cup of coffee and began to talk about all sorts of psychic happenings and phenomena. It must have been about 11.30 pm on the 25th when we started to speak; by 1.00 am, we were in the presence of something astonishing, something vast, something incredibly intelligent.

It began simply. I asked whether the tingles or goosebumps we feel when moved by a beautiful piece of music or poem could be a link to the 'great beyond'. The response was immediate, and Catherine and I looked at each other in total shock. As soon as I had finished my sentence, colossal amounts of 'tingles' travelled like waves through our bodies, so much so that tears were running down our faces. The tears were not caused by emotion; they were caused by the sheer power of the energy that now enwrapped and penetrated our souls. We were, it seemed, submerged and saturated by God. I was shaking, but there was such a feeling of peace. And I didn't want to let this idyllic state slip by without savouring its sweetness.

Mysticism, the 'tingles' seemed to confirm, resulted from man's conscious need for communion with God. Painting, sculpting, poetry, and music are all based on man's need for beauty and have a close relationship with the divine. Everything else in mysticism grows out of this.

The 'tingles' kept getting stronger; so strong that we now called the sensation 'electricity'. It was like being pleasantly electrocuted, and we were both feeling the same thing. Electricity, of course, is not just something you buy in a battery. It is one of the basic ingredients of the universe. And the 'electricity' Catherine and I were experiencing was conscious; it had a mind.

I could give many examples of what happened throughout that morning to illustrate this consciousness, but I shall make do with just one. It must have been around 4.30 am. We had already discovered that we could pull this energy through our bodies (actually feeling it pass through) and that it could respond to thoughts and queries. However, when Catherine said, "I wish Walter (her husband) could experience this", the power of the electricity was almost too much to bear. I was lucky. I was sitting in an armchair at the time, but Catherine was standing, and it threw her off her feet. It was incredible and, as I describe it, I realise once again that I can't describe it.

So much occurred during that morning, including a cobalt blue light about the size of a baseball that moved along the apex of the wall at speed, stopped, and then vanished. I could write an entire book on what occurred on 26 January 1983, but that's not what 'this' book is about. Suffice to say that when the energy faded, a little after 9.00 am, Catherine and I went for a walk, feeling light and elated. We left the house and walked out into a different world, a much more pleasant world. The sun was shining brightly, and everything looked fresh and new. Nothing would ever be the same again.

Of course, many people have had similar experiences, one being heavy rocker Brian Welch. Some of you will have heard of the American heavy metal band Korn, which has sold over fifty million albums worldwide. I freely admit I hadn't and have never heard of a note of their music, but these boys are heavy rockers and very, very successful. Yet, one of its founder members, Brian Welch, found God, and the way he did so is of interest to this book.

Brian had a young daughter, Jeanea, who had lost her mom to drugs. He was heavily into various substances, too – in fact, in the world he operated in, it was almost expected of him. Known around the world to his friends and fans as 'Head', he had made it big – multi-platinum big – as co-founder and lead guitarist of Korn. So he perhaps surprised himself when he cried out to God.

He had become torn. He wanted to care for his daughter and hated exposing her to the wild party life of Korn. He has been quoted as saying, "How can you leave a huge band that's like one of the biggest bands that's come around, rock bands, that changed music, how can you leave that? But how can I not be there for my daughter?"

As Brian agonised over this decision, he drove deeper and deeper into drugs and alcohol. One day, he heard his daughter singing a Korn song. These are not nursery rhymes, and this particular song revolved around dreaming about sex all day long. Naturally, this hit him hard; children shouldn't be singing songs like that.

After receiving an email from a friend and business colleague who knew he was in trouble, which quoted the Gospel of Matthew - "Come to me, all you who are weary and I will give you rest"- Brian began to ask if Jesus could be real.

After a bit of investigation, he ended up visiting a church, even saying a prayer, "'Lord, if you're real like that guy says, please take these drugs from me. I can't quit, I don't want to do them, but I can't stop. I want to be here for Jeanea. She lost her mom to drugs. I need your help. Just help me. Help, help me, God." He said it from the heart.

Brian snorted 'speed' and read the Bible for a week, searching for answers. Then something amazing happened. "I felt this peaceful presence, and I started shaking a little bit, and I got goosebumps everywhere. And the first thing I felt was 'I love you.' And I was like, 'Father?' I was frozen. 'Father?' This was God, and then it went away. But it was so real. It took over the high. And when it went away, the drugs said, 'that's just drugs. That's not real'. So I did drugs all night long. And the next day, I woke up, and I had the feeling to go to my Bible. I opened it up and pointed: 'the soul who sins is the soul who dies'. And to me, right then, it was like God told me I revealed myself to you last night. It's time for you to stop the drugs. It's time for you to be done. And I was consumed with fear, and I went and grabbed all my drugs and threw them in the toilet, and I said, 'I'm done, God. I'm yours now. I'm yours'. That's the last time I did drugs."

Brian considers it a miracle that he could get clean after being addicted to narcotics for so long. It's hard to disagree.

An Iranian man by the name of Khosrow has also felt the energy or electricity. As a young man, he entered an Assyrian Christian church to try and find 'some answers'. Inside, an elderly priest gave him several books to read. They were all in Farsi, and among them was a copy of the New Testament, which Khosrow read from cover to cover. However, reading alone was unable to satisfy his search, and he found himself tossing the book against a wall in anger.

As he did so, a man came to him in a vision and, extending his hands toward Khosrow, said, "Take my hands, and everything will change forever." Khosrow took the man's hands and a wave of what he describes as 'electricity' flowed through his body.

Today, many years later, Khosrow is fond of telling how he was once asked by a sceptic how he could be so sure that the vision wasn't a product of his imagination. Khosrow asked the sceptic if he was wearing clothes. The man was taken aback by the question, but the analogy was clear. Khosrow's vision was as real, perhaps more so.

Susie Benford was a phenomenal woman. As a child, she almost died from cancer, surviving it but dealing with multiple handicaps. Yet, she achieved many things that she was just not supposed to. These included becoming the strongest woman in the world (three-time World Power-lifting Champion and holder of every single World Record in the 97lb weight class), a registered nurse, health care researcher, and Executive Director of a non-profit biomedical organisation in Ohio. Her incredible thirst for knowledge also led to the in-depth study of religion and the scientific testing of unexplained phenomena, such as the Shroud of Turin.

In Susie's book 'Strong Woman', she tells the entire story of her life, an incredible life that led to a long series of dreams and visions in which she communicated with the apostle John and Jesus.

I admit that I have a lot of trouble coming to terms with some of Susie's proclamations, but that does not mean she's not right. Strong Woman is worth a read, whether you are interested in the teachings of Jesus, the Shroud of Turin, or merely phenomena we cannot understand. It's a book that makes you think, even if you don't hold with all of its conclusions.

I am one hundred per cent sure that Susie experienced something authentic. The reason for this revolves around a section of the book where, having discovered the existence of a work entitled The Gnostic Gospels, she heads off to retrieve it from the bookstore. I shall let Susie tell the story:

"On my way, I started to get a strange feeling. It was as if there was some kind of electrical current running through my body. This was something that I had never felt before. I was at a loss to explain where this weird and sudden sensation had come from.

"As I arrived at the bookstore and walked up to the 'books on hold' counter, the sensation intensified. The clerk was busy with another customer and stood, with his back to me, about ten feet away. There were over a hundred books on the shelves above, awaiting the arrival of purchasers.

"As I gazed over the groupings of indistinguishable books, I felt a swishing current go through me. Almost simultaneously, the clerk shuddered as if he were having a slight seizure of some sort. Immediately after that, one solitary book fell from its shelved position with a loud thud.

"The book was The Gnostic Gospels."

It sounds like a story out of Harry Potter, but I can assure you that this energy, electricity, is real. Once you've experienced it, it is the most natural thing in the world. And I do not doubt that whatever is controlling this energy would have no trouble at all in 'pushing' a book onto the floor.

People often ask if I would like to go through that mystical experience again. Of course! I have to say, though, that this 'consciousness' has never really left me. It's true that it has never been as strong as that night in January 1983, or stayed for anything like eight hours, more like thirty seconds or a minute nowadays. It is still present, however, and it still communicates in a very subtle way. No prophecies or big proclamations; instead, support and a feeling that I am not alone in life's darkest moments. No-one is.

Yet how best to describe a mystical experience when, by its very nature, it is indescribable? The Hindu tradition of Advaita Vedanta utilises a parable to describe such 'peak' experiences, as psychologists would term them. Imagine being in a dark room. You have been told that in this room lives an enormous snake. As you sit in the room, you can see its silhouette and feel great dread as you ponder the potential for it to attack you at any moment. But one day, there is a burst of light that illuminates the room, and you see that what looked like a snake is, in reality, a rope. Although the flash of light was fleeting, it gave you a glimpse of the truth. All of a sudden, your long-held fear dissolved entirely, and your experience in the room was never the same again. This is what a mystical encounter feels like: it is a flash of truth that frees you from your limited sense of self and gives you a taste of a reality that somehow appears more real.

Touching the Divine

"If there is anyone who owes everything to Bach, it is certainly God."
Emil Cioran

When I recall the eight-hour mystical experience of 1983, I can't help but note that it began in response to my comment that the 'tingles' started when listening to a beautiful piece of music or poetry. In my case, that beautiful music is often by Johann Sebastian Bach (1685-1750).

When I hear the music of J.S. Bach, I get an insight into the workings of the Universe, or (as Bach himself would doubtless prefer to say) into the mind of God.

Even if they have never heard a note of his music (which is unlikely in the Western world), most people have heard of J.S. Bach, arguably the most famous and gifted of all composers. Despite this, many do not know that this inspired composer was also a theologian committed to God. He studied scripture thoroughly and, at the age of forty-eight, acquired Luther's three-volume translation of the Bible. He underlined passages, corrected errors in the text and commentary, inserted missing words, and made notes in the margin. Perhaps it should come as no surprise, therefore, that he also became known as 'the Fifth Evangelist', having an extraordinary influence in leading the spiritually thirsty to Christianity.

"Music's only purpose should be the glory of God and the recreation of the human spirit," Bach proclaimed. In doing so, he explained the 'why' behind our diverse vocations, talents, and careers: they are for the help and enlightenment of our fellow man and God, not for ourselves. With this in mind, the next time you listen to a work by Bach, reflect on what that music is saying, even the secular pieces. His life and example changed innumerable lives and is still changing lives all over the world today.

When asked what message he would choose to send from Earth into outer space in the Voyager spacecraft, eminent biologist and author Lewis Thomas replied, "I would send the complete works of Johann Sebastian Bach." After a pause, he added, "but that would be boasting."

If one considers the subject deeply enough, no thinking person can deny the divinity of music, the language of the soul. It has the power to bring people together all over the world, not just man to man, but also man to God.

From the metaphysical standpoint, nothing can touch the formless except for the art of music, which in itself is formless. Some mystics believe that the innermost being of man is the Akasha. In Hinduism, this means the basis and essence of all things in the material world. It is one of the Panchamahabhuta, or 'five elements'(the other four being Air, Fire, Water, and Earth), and its principal characteristic is Shabda (sound). Another point of view is that all creation came from vibrations, which the Hindus have called Nada. In the Bible, we can find it as the 'Word', which came first of all.

On this point, all of the various religions come together. Man, therefore, loves music more than anything else. Music is his nature, it has come from vibrations, and he himself is vibration. Hazrat Inayat Khan expresses this thoroughly and eloquently in his book, The Music of Life: 'Like all the mysteries of the spirit, the answers are always there and instantaneously on hand; we need only be awakened. Music possesses the power to awaken.'

Perhaps this is why to an Indian, music is not merely an amusement or for entertainment. It is something more. It responds to the deepest yearnings of the soul. "Music alone can take you to the Highest!" said Swami Vivekananda, Sri Ramakrishna's foremost disciple and the man who is primarily responsible for bringing the wisdom and teachings of India's Vedanta philosophy to the West.

Music is indeed mystical in a very real sense. It allows the listener to remain completely alert to what they can't see, rather than being fixated on what they can see, such as words on a page or pictures on a television screen. It is not always easy to understand the effect that music has upon us. The American composer Aaron Copland explained it all perfectly: "The whole problem can be stated quite simply by asking: 'Is there a meaning to music?' My answer to that would be, 'Yes'. And 'Can you state in so many words what the meaning is?' My answer to that would be, 'No'."

In the spring of 2005, the Paris-based artist Katia Eliad was suffering from a severe creative block. She was at an artistic dead-end, and for some inexplicable reason, unable to use green or blue in her abstract paintings. Katia could have sought out a therapist or even visited her doctor for a few pills. She did neither. Instead, she opted for a rather odd treatment: daily two-hour sessions of Mozart's music for three weeks at a time.

Filtering the music through special vibrating headphones that sometimes cut out the lowest tones, the impact, she says, was remarkable: "I'm much more at ease with myself, with people, with everything. It feels like I've done ten years of psychoanalysis in just eight months." As for Mozart, "he's become like a grandfather who calms you when you wake up in the middle of a nightmare." Blue and green are now back in her palette.

The composer John Tavener described his personal view of Mozart in terms that are clearly spiritual, explaining: "I believe that Mozart's soul apprehended the theophany that came to him from God. Unconsciously no doubt Mozart's soul became aware of the ecstatic vision bestowed upon him. It was a vision that he could never have explained or understood in words, but a vision nonetheless that his soul would continuously pour forth in music."

He said that the 'sacredness' he associates with Mozart could also be found in Persian and Hindu miniature paintings. Tavener believed that Mozart was the most natural composer that ever lived. And Mozart's music, he suggested, pre-existed. And this is, perhaps, the crux of our argument: maybe great art is never really composed, written, or painted. Instead, it is 'plucked out of the ether' by those creative souls with some link to the divine. Initially, for example, when we hear the beautiful 'Et in carnatus est' from the C minor Mass, we hear music by God but written down by Mozart. And the electricity we have discussed is recognition of this fact – music (and the other arts) is in a genuine sense divine.

There is no doubt in my mind that great art acts as a portal to higher consciousness. Such art propels the psyche to places it had not previously experienced, to epiphanies. As E.T.A. Hoffman wrote in his 'Essay on Beethoven': "Music opens to man an unknown region, a world that has nothing in common with the world that surrounds him, in which he leaves behind all ordinary feeling to surrender himself to an inexpressible longing."

The Chinese Text 'The Spring and Autumn Annals, written in 722BCE, states: "The origin of music lies far back in time. It arises out of harmony, and it is rooted in the Great One (the Holy Spirit). The Great One gives rise to two poles: the two poles give rise to the powers of darkness and light. That from which all beings arise and in which they have their origin is the Great One; that whereby they form and perfect themselves is the duality of darkness and light. As soon as the seed-germs start to stir, they coagulate into a form. The bodily shape belongs to the world of space, and everything special has a sound. The sound arises out of harmony. Harmony arises out of relatedness. Harmony and relatedness are the roots from which music, established by the ancient kings, arose."

There are 'modern' tunes that one could easily argue have been divinely inspired, too. One of the most famous examples is that of Yesterday, penned by Paul McCartney. According to the Guinness Book of Records, one of the world's most well-known songs, the song with the most cover versions, Yesterday, came to the ex-Beatle in a dream. He woke up with the tune in his head, he said, and immediately decided to play it. "I got out of bed, sat at the piano, found G, found F sharp minor 7th - and that leads you through then to B to E minor, and finally back to E. It all leads forward logically. I liked the melody a lot, but because I'd dreamed it, I couldn't believe I'd written it. I thought, 'No, I've never written anything like this before.' But I had the tune, which was the most magic thing!"

He was still uncertain whether he had repeated someone else's song, so he played it to anyone who would listen, but no one could identify it. Numerous fans have tried to do the same. Perhaps they're looking in the wrong place.

Of course, it is not only the arts where this great creative source is active. Many scientists have spoken of a mystical element when pursuing solutions to particularly thorny problems. Some claim that much of Isaac Newton's theoretical system developed from a mystical experience and spiritual study.

Isaac Newton was an intensely religious person, but with a personal secret belief considered heretical at his time - he did not believe in the Trinity. He thought it a blasphemy. However, he was very interested in Gnosticism, and some claim he achieved his scientific results from his studies of Gnostic writings. Whether you believe this or not, it is impossible to look at Newton's life and discoveries without considering the fact that he was a secret religious heretic. He was deeply interested in the source of all things, and perhaps, given his undoubted scientific success, the 'source of all things' was interested in him too. Newton was open to possibilities, which is vital in the realm of mystical experience; even if you don't consciously open the door to such things, you need to keep the door unlocked.

That is why poets and writers have described the instantaneous nature of inspiration in which the entire conception or idea or story is grasped, which would usually require months of working out through rational, empirical means.

The American poet Ruth Stone has explained how she received inspiration for her poetry. When she was growing up in rural Virginia, she would be out working in the fields and said that she could actually feel and hear a poem coming at her from over the landscape. She described it as being like a thunderous train of air; it would come barrelling down at her. Ruth said that when she felt it coming – because it would shake the earth under her feet - she knew that she had only one thing to do at that point, and that was to, in her words, "run like hell". She did this all the way to the house in which she lived, being chased by a poem. When inside, she had to get to a piece of paper and a pencil fast enough so that when it thundered through her, she could gather it and write it on the page.

It's essential always to be open to such inspiration. As the artist, Philip Guston, said, "I go to my studio every day because one day I may go and the Angel will be there. What if I don't go and the Angel came?"

The question is, why are artists, and all other creative people, so different in so many ways? And if divine inspiration makes itself apparent in artists in their behaviour, what form does it take in the actual art? Can it be recognised?

A word that 16th-century (and later) writers sometimes use to identify that extra special something in a work of art is 'grazia' (grace). Very difficult to define, it can be described as something added to beauty, but not directly visible. It has a mysterious quality (the source for that feeling you get when you stand in front of a great work of art and feel those 'tingles') and is associated with divine inspiration. A work of art is believed to contain an extra indefinable spiritual essence.

At the end of the day, though, it defies analysis. Indeed, in 17th-century France, it was referred to as 'un non so che' (I-don't-know-what), a precursor to 'je-ne-sais-quoi'.

TDC Without Technology

"Next to a circus, there ain't nothing that packs up and tears out any quicker than the Christmas spirit."
Kin Hubbard

The Austro-Bavarian fable of Krampus, the shadow of Saint Nicholas, otherwise known as Santa Claus, is about a horned creature that beats naughty children or carries them off with his razor-sharp claws. Saint Nicholas rewards the virtuous child; Krampus punishes the wicked. I had obviously been rather naughty during 2005 because Krampus paid me a Christmas Day visit.

At the time, I lived in an old Victorian terrace house in the heart of a small Staffordshire village. For that reason, if nothing else, I was determined to produce a traditional Victorian Christmas, an old-fashioned Christmas, one that encapsulated the spirit of Tiny Tim and Scrooge's cheery nephew Bob Cratchit. And I use the word 'produce' advisably. This was indeed a production: a natural (and ridiculously large) tree, a roaring fire, mistletoe and ivy, enough food and drink to feed every single one of Santa's little helpers, a sizeable mound of presents, and 'Hark the Herald Angels Sing' playing on the hi-fi.

It should be noted that I didn't just want this to be a Christmas driven by shopping and food either. I wanted a more profound experience. Over the past fifty years or so, commercial interests have, to a significant degree, hijacked Santa Claus in the interest of selling 'things'. Before that, Santa Claus, aka St. Nicholas, remained more spiritually meaningful. I wanted this particular festive season to have some real meaning, but without taking the fun away. However, while I wanted a spiritually-infused

Christmas with a visit from St. Nicholas and his reindeer, what I got was a visit from Krampus and a couple of paramedics.

Now I may be building this up to some major seasonal event. Despite this, it was not to be a huge gathering, just my fiancée, Diane, two very close friends, Heather and Colin, and my mother, Barbara, who had celebrated her eightieth birthday earlier that year. Lunch was planned for around 2.00 pm. It was just turned 11.00 am, and everything was going to plan. Then the telephone rang.

It was my mother's sister, who informed me that they had just been talking on the telephone when "your mom's voice went all funny, she was talking nonsense, and then I think she dropped the phone. Now I can't get back in touch with her."

Diane and I drove over to my mother's house at considerable speed. I was trying to stay positive, but deep down I knew something was very, very wrong. I realised on some level that those precious hours when you discover your parents' stories and unlock treasured memories were to be no more.

When we arrived at my mother's bungalow, we could see her through the front window sitting in a chair, immobile. She was conscious but seemingly paralysed. The door was locked. The back door, I could see, though, was open, and so I broke down the fence that led to the rear garden and forced my way into the property. It immediately became apparent that my mother had had a stroke; she looked terrified, didn't seem to be able to move, and spoke in a series of numbers, meaningless words, and phrases: "Sixty-two, forty-four, yes and no, I think yesterday, tooty-two."

Considering it was Christmas Day, the ambulance arrived quickly, and the paramedics were exceptional. We followed the ambulance to Queen's Hospital in Burton-on-

Trent, and it was here that we began to realise that this was the wrong day to be taken ill.

When Ludwig van Beethoven was fifty-six, returning in an open wagon from his brother's estate, he caught pneumonia and never fully recovered. Late in the afternoon on 26 March 1827, Ludwig lay ill in his bed. A storm was forming outside. The sky darkened. Lightning lit up Beethoven's room, and a loud thunderclap filled the air. Beethoven opened his eyes, raised his fist, and fell back dead. Or so the story goes.

The events in Queen's Hospital were not quite so dramatic, but the level of care and technology would have been easily recognisable to residents of early 19th-century Vienna. For almost two hours, we sat in a cubicle without seeing hardly anyone, certainly not a doctor. At one stage, a nurse did hook my mother up to a blood pressure monitor, which I recall reading 220/180, but that was it. As any teenager will tell you, horror games work best in a totally immersive environment, and this hospital certainly provided that.

Looking back now, I realise that if my mother had been taken ill in Germany, Italy, or France, things would have turned out differently. But this was England. I don't think I need to explain any further. The people you think you can turn to when things go bad didn't respond. The system let my mother down, and no doubt countless other mothers over the years. And it was the 'system' – the doctors and nurses were, and are, magnificent, but they are working with their hands tied behind their backs, putting up with bad government and too many people in suits.

My mother remained in Queen's Hospital for precisely a week before being transferred to a smaller 'cottage' hospital around fifteen miles away. Those seven days were difficult; we thought we had lost her more than once. On the rare occasions she was conscious and tried to speak, she made little sense. However, because of my experience of TDC, I knew that these incoherent ramblings were not the complete story. With this in mind, on the fourth day she was in the hospital, I took in a recording device. She didn't say much, but via TDC, she proclaimed, *"My guest is Cathy."* I didn't realise until after I had studied the recording that the nurse looking after my mother that day was named Cathy, something I noticed when I saw her name badge the following day. My mother had brain damage and couldn't possibly have seen the nurse's name badge without her spectacles anyway, but on some level, she knew, and that level had nothing to do with the human brain.

Within weeks, everyone realised that it would have been far kinder if she had have passed over in those first few days. But it was a hell that was just beginning. It would be more than two-and-a-half years before she finally made that journey to the 'unknown country'.

She stayed in the cottage hospital for three months after her stroke, during which time she suffered a second stroke, which more or less killed off any chink of light that may have existed. She was now so brain-damaged it was impossible to communicate with her. To all intents and purposes, my mother had gone.

Despite this, upon her being discharged, I decided not to put her into a nursing home, a route I had been advised to take by social workers, friends, relatives, and the man on the corner who sells fruit and veg. No one thought it was a good idea, but I decided to do a little work on her bungalow so that I could care for her in her own home. I had a conservatory built with views of the fields at the rear of the property, and a wet room was installed, the kitchen gutted, and everywhere else refurbished. She hated it.

I say she hated it, but that probably wasn't entirely true. I was told that people who have major strokes often act in precisely the opposite manner to when they were fit and well. Throughout her life, my mother was a gentle, kind soul, happy with her lot. The family was her big thing, and animals, particularly her cats. She was always cheerful and had a smile on her face. I guess you can imagine the opposite of that.

Of course, she wasn't always in a foul temper. But she was constantly frustrated and desperately unhappy. Every time she went to bed, she cried her heart out. Every morning, she yelled for help, wanting to get out of bed. Paralysed from the waist down, she was being held prisoner in her own body. I had to toilet her too, something no child should ever have to do for his parents.

I recall one period, when to add to the stress and emotional pain, I hurt my back, picking my mother up off the floor (she fell out of her chair on several occasions). In a great deal of pain, I couldn't even sit or lay down. One sultry summer's evening, I remember being in the back garden, trying to sleep leaning against the bungalow wall. I was in physical agony, emotional turmoil, and my blood pressure was touching 185/115. Then I started itching all over. This drove me crazy for months, but it was all the result of trying to cope with something I could not cope with. I was in overload.

Friends and family again suggested I place my mother in a home. At first, I fought against this suggestion. But eventually, I could see that my mother would be better somewhere with nurses and dedicated carers. This blinding light on the road to Damascus occurred four months after taking on the role of sole carer.

Over six million people are acting as carers for a friend or relative in the UK. It can be a heart-breaking process, seeing someone you love suffer enormous distress day after day. The whole thing can be time-consuming, physically and emotionally demanding, and impacts significantly on your finances. Yet, one remarkable thing did happen during this period.

It was the week before she died and, as I entered the main room of the nursing home, the residents were all slumped in chairs pushed up against the walls, a depressing example of how the elderly and infirm are treated in the UK. I stayed with my mother for around an hour, telling her the latest news and asking her how lunch was, none of which resulted in any recognition at all on her part. It never did. As I moved to leave, I pushed the chair I was using back into its place against the wall and crouched down to say goodbye. "I'll see you tomorrow," I said. Then the most incredible thing happened. My mother suddenly smiled (something she hadn't done for two-and-a-half years), leaned forwards and said, "I love you."

I was dumbstruck. The doctors had said her brain was far too damaged for communication in any real sense, and she hadn't uttered a word since before the second stroke. It was impossible. But it happened. Nonetheless, that moment of lucidity vanished as quickly as it came. Immediately after saying what she had to say, my mother fell back into a primarily vegetative state. Yet for an instant, she had returned; but what had returned? Medical science says it is not possible that it was her brain, so was it her soul overriding the brain before death? Many people may find this a far-fetched idea, but it is the only reasonable, logical one that remains.

My mother's soul had pushed through her worn-out and dying body, using it one last time to speak to her son. Moreover, this kind of event is surprisingly common, so common that I have a second example of 'the sunshine hour' in my own family.

I was not present on this occasion but have been told this story by my father and grandfather, both grounded men, engineers by trade, who needed evidence to accept any theory whatsoever. So I tend to believe them.

It was October 1964, and my grandmother, Ivy, was in bed at home with cancer that had spread throughout her body. For most of the last week of her life, she remained unconscious, the drugs easing her pain and forcing her to sleep. The morning of the day she died, though, my grandfather, Harry, and my father's brother, Eric, were sitting beside the bed when Ivy suddenly opened her eyes and smiled, saying, "Nellie came to visit me last night. There were so many stairs. But she's coming back to help me tonight." Nellie was Ivy's mother-in-law, my grandfather's mother, who had died just four years earlier.

I have no real idea of the response from my grandfather and Eric, but they probably put it down to some kind of hallucination caused by her illness or the drugs. Nevertheless, that evening the family had gathered around her bed; my father, grandfather, and Eric were all present. At around 7.30 pm, Ivy opened her eyes for a second time. She was weary, and with a gentle smile, she announced, "Nellie is here. I go now." And with that, she closed her eyes and made her transition without delay.

Again, out of unconsciousness arose great lucidity. She had returned briefly to inform her husband and sons that it was time to leave, that she was going on a journey. This seems intended to ease the grief of those who loved her, similar to when my mother said: "I love you." Nellie had come to collect her, and it is as if she was saying, "It's okay, I'm leaving this worn-out body, but I'll still exist, I'll see you again. Don't worry."

Many people who have had a severely damaged brain, either through Alzheimer's, stroke, dementia, cancer, or other conditions, seem to have the ability to 'return', and that return is unequivocally driven by love.

When the brain dies, the person who hosted it vanishes into non-existence forever. At least, that's what conventional science says. Once a brain is ravaged by a disease such as Alzheimer's, there is no coming back, and there is zero chance of improvement. Yet, for those close to death, that is not always the case.

This fact was first brought to my attention in early 2007 when a friend's elderly mother, Elsie, who no longer recognised her loved ones and never spoke, suddenly astonished her daughter when she smiled and thanked her for everything she had done. She then held a conversation with her daughter for around fifteen minutes, during which time she told her how much she loved her and asked her to pass on her love to her grandchildren and other family members and friends. She then went quiet again and could recognise no one. That evening she passed away in the nursing home she had lived in for the past four years.

According to reductionist science, this is not possible. The fact is that her brain's cerebral cortex and hippocampus, necessary for memory, thought, and language, had severely shrunk. There was a minimal resemblance between Elsie's brain and a healthy brain. Yet it happened. She was able to communicate with great clarity for approximately a quarter of an hour. Similar cases are scattered throughout the medical literature.

One concerns a nun who went 'crazy' after a bout of scarlet fever, suddenly recovering after three years of mental instability. At the same time as her scarlet fever, she became increasingly debilitated physically. Fascinatingly, the more her physical state declined, the saner she became. Just before her death, she became entirely rational and coherent. In the subsequent autopsy of her brain, it was discovered that the brain was so swollen that as soon as the skull was cut, it forced itself out, and it was impossible to put it back in again.

Similarly, sufferers of meningitis (swelling of the membrane of the brain and spinal cord) have experienced astonishing recoveries that defy explanation given the severe impairment caused by the condition. A good illustration of this concerns a woman who lost her cognition and memory due to a chronic meningitis infection. To everyone's amazement, she began to regain her memories and lucidity as her body continued to decline. Just before her death, she had become fully sentient. As with the nun, the autopsy revealed acute swelling and considerable excess fluid in her skull, in addition to blisters covering the membrane and other sections of the brain.

A woman who had had Alzheimer's disease for nine years and could no longer recognise even her son, suddenly, the day before her passing, regained not only recognition of her family but also knowledge of things she hadn't seemed to have been aware of up to that time. This included her age and where she had been living the final years of her life.

An increasing number of researchers, including Bruce Greyson, Professor of Psychiatry and Neurobehavioral Sciences at the University of Virginia, and Michael Nahm in Freiburg, Germany, have a name for the state that the nun and others find themselves in before death – terminal lucidity. It appears that normal cognition does occur despite a severely damaged brain, not often, but, for instance, in something like 5-10% of Alzheimer's cases. And only when death is very near.

How can this happen? We know that there is no observable transformation in the brain. The cerebral cortex (the relatively thin, folded, outer 'grey matter' layer of the brain crucial for thinking, information processing, memory, and attention) doesn't unexpectedly grow billions of new neurons. So what accounts for terminal lucidity in Alzheimer's patients?

The most logical answer, and one that is now progressively more accepted by open-minded scientists and medical professionals, is that the short-term return to lucidity just before death is brought about, not by some incomprehensible surge in brain functioning, but by the mind distancing itself from the brain.

Think about how a radio picks up signals and converts them into music coming out of your radio. This is a good analogy of how the mind and brain interact, the brain being the radio. If a receiver is damaged somehow, it will stop working. It is identical to the relationship between mind and brain; if the brain is damaged, the information it filters will become less coherent. It's a similar process.

In any event, terminal lucidity, what the New York Times chose to call an 'end-of-life rally', and the Victorians called 'lightning before death', is well-known. What is not well-known is how long that clarity lasts. Not every case is the same, with 'rallies' lasting anything from a few moments to a couple of months, occasionally enough time to take a break from the care home or hospice and return home. However long the rally lasts, though, most patients are searching for closure and saying their goodbyes. Some palliative care experts describe patients who request weird and wonderful meals or the presence of someone to pay their last respects, and these specific requests show the patient's awareness of the fact that they will be passing over in the not too distant future.

As a woman on BBC Radio 4's 'Out of the Ordinary' explained when talking of how her mother, who had had a brain tumour and whose communication was minimal, suddenly woke up and sang in the hospice, "We joined in and held her hand. It was a magical moment that myself and my dad had. We hadn't had that connection for a while. It was beautiful."

In the field of terminal lucidity, Professor Alexander Batthyány is a pioneering researcher, a man who follows curiosity wherever it leads him.

Born in 1971, Batthyány is the Viktor Frankl Professor of Philosophy and Psychology in Liechtenstein and teaches at the Department for Cognition Sciences at the University of Vienna and the Vienna University Clinic for Psychiatry. Since 2012, he has also been a Guest Professor for Existential Psychology in Moscow. Also, the author of numerous publications, he is undertaking the first large study into terminal lucidity.

This study primarily takes the form of a detailed questionnaire, which he sends out to caregivers, mostly nurses and doctors, of those people who have died of Alzheimer's disease. The results have continued to be fascinating, seemingly throwing up new mysteries and puzzles with every questionnaire returned.

Batthyány's results are increasingly suggesting that normal cognition does occur despite a severely damaged brain; not often, but enough to make it a genuine phenomenon. Batthyány describes it as being "close to a miracle, given what we know about brain function and cognition."

Conventional brain science has no explanation. The return of mental clarity and memory in a brain devastated by Alzheimer's is not supposed to happen. Yet it does. And it changes lives. One of Batthyany's respondents confessed how she used to think of her advanced Alzheimer's patients as 'human vegetables'. An isolated occurrence of terminal lucidity changed her mind. "Had you seen what I saw, you could understand that dementia can affect the soul but not destroy it. I only wish I had known this earlier."

It is now well over a decade since the study began, with Batthyany having encountered more than two hundred cases, which he believes points to a much more significant and widespread trend.

A good case-in-point is Mary Dunn, a ninety-three-year-old woman at Cornwall Park Hospital in Auckland, New Zealand. Kate Burnett, a staff member, said that Mary was frequently bad-tempered, shouting, and cursing at hospital employees. So it came as somewhat of a surprise that Kate arrived one morning to discover that Mary was asking for her. Straightaway, she could tell something had changed. "In fact, Mary's features were very different, soft and loving," Kate told the Daily Mirror. "Her usual colourful language was replaced with words of kindness and joy."

That wasn't all, though. Mary's memories had returned. She told Kate about her life and even had a personal message for her: "She apologised for the way she spoke to the carers and to me," Kate explained, "and thanked the entire team for their compassion despite her unkind words."

Nevertheless, later the same day, Mary's lucidity came to an end and once again, she became hostile. Even so, the experience changed Kate's outlook. "I know that deep down in that dementia patient is a vibrant, intelligent, and loving woman," she said. "It was such a gift - really a miracle."

The late Austrian-American philosopher Paul Edwards, who died in 2004, published an article entitled 'Alzheimer's Argument Against the Soul' in 1995. In the article, he used the example of Mrs D, a kind-hearted and charitable woman before the commencement of the disease. The disease so brutally corrupted her brain that she began physically assaulting other patients in the hospital in later years. Edwards assumed that Mrs D's extreme change in personality was strong evidence that the brain must generate the mind. As Mrs D's brain function declined, a comparable deterioration in lucidity and rational thought resulted. Consequently, the brain, he suggested, must produce the mind within it and, as a result, be reliant on the brain for effective functioning.

Dr Batthyany uses Edward's example of Mrs D to ask a different question: What if "much like the moon eclipses the sun, the brain eclipses the self?" Is it possible that an Alzheimer's patient's severely damaged brain restricts the consciousness and distorts the personality but does not intrinsically harm the mind behind it? In a similar way that a broken radio provides only snippets of garbled speech, while the radio signals behind it remain clear and undamaged, the soul remains healthy and complete as the brain disintegrates.

Maybe in this brief period preceding death, consciousness begins to disengage from the brain, allowing the true self, the eternal soul, to shine through like a ray of sunshine.

So could these inexplicable moments of lucidity be genuinely miraculous? Marilyn Mendoza, a psychologist and a clinical instructor in psychiatry at Tulane University Medical Centre, commented: "There's no scientific reason for these moments of lucidity at present, and I think a part of that is because it's more of a spiritual experience. For family members, these moments can have a more immediate effect on a spiritual level."

It increasingly looks like the brain does not create consciousness, which poses a significant problem for materialists and reductionist science. And the more science examines the problem, the more the 'transceiver' theory - where we understand the source of consciousness as non-physical – becomes the go-to solution. Put simply, research into the relationship between consciousness and the brain indicates that the origin of 'self' is metaphysical and not biological, even though it communicates back and forth through the intermediary of the brain while the host body is still alive.

This theory has become so popular that even leading scientists in neurology are sitting up and taking note. This is because new information points to capacities of will and consciousness that defy any existing physiological model. That even includes explanations suggested through quantum physics. Various scientists have concluded that there is no prospect of any future physiological model showing that human consciousness is the random product of neurological activity.

Terminal lucidity, deathbed visions, and near-death experiences can all occur when brains are severely damaged, when people have no apparent biological or medical ability to talk or act. What's more, brains that have been examined after the death of patients who experienced terminal lucidity show no physical improvement or change in their condition.

On the All Nurses forum, hospice nurses report terminal lucidity as a common occurrence, with one commenting: "Seen it a zillion times, patient in bad shape, get in report, patient doing better, awake, eating, etc., and we know that the end is near."

Another says, "I can't count the number of times I've seen this phenomenon. The most recent was a couple of weeks ago when a comatose patient I'd cared for several times suddenly woke up, looked at his wife and family gathered around, smiled and said a few words. They thought it was a miracle. I tried gently to discourage this thinking, but to no avail, and they were genuinely shocked when he slipped back into the coma and died an hour later."

Science has no explanation for any of these 'recoveries'. The only real rationalisation of this phenomenon is that there is more to the human mind than just its brain physiology. And I would suggest that terminal lucidity cases are examples of brain-free consciousness; the soul is freeing itself from the physical body and limitations of the damaged brain as death approaches.

The point is that all of this is a form of TDC without the need for technology. The human soul will always find a way to communicate if it needs to, whether using a poorly wired and corrupted human brain or a laptop computer. These little miracles happen every day of the week in every country and city in the world, yet not many people notice. Their lives are more impoverished for that.

Prayer Helps You

"In prayer, it is better to have a heart without words than words without a heart."
John Bunyan

Whether or not prayer works is an essential question for the spiritually oriented. When we talk with God, does he hear us? Some people will try to persuade you that science disproves prayer, but nothing could be further from the truth.

Numerous scientific studies have been conducted to show that prayer has a positive effect. A 1993 Israeli study, for instance, followed ten thousand civil servants for twenty-six years and discovered that Orthodox Jews were less likely to die of heart issues than 'non-believers'. Furthermore, a 1995 study from Dartmouth College in Hanover, New Hampshire, monitored two hundred and fifty people following open-heart surgery and found that those who had religious convictions and social support were twelve times less likely to die than agnostics and atheists.

In the most widely publicised research on the effect of intercessory prayer, cardiologist Randolph Byrd studied three hundred and ninety-three patients admitted to the coronary care unit at San Francisco General Hospital. A number were prayed for by home prayer groups; others were not. Every one of the men and women involved in the study received medical treatment. In this randomised, double-blind study, neither the hospital staff nor the patients knew who would be the focus of prayer. The outcome was extraordinary and astonished quite a few scientists. Those whose medical treatment was supplemented with prayer required fewer drugs and spent a shorter period on ventilators. They did better in the long run than their peers, who received medical attention but no prayers. Patients who were prayed for were much less likely to require antibiotics (three patients versus sixteen); significantly less likely to develop pulmonary oedema (six versus eighteen); and considerably less likely to need insertion of a tube into the throat to help with breathing (zero versus twelve).

A survey conducted by the Pew Research Centre found that just over half of scientists (51%) have faith in some form of deity or higher power; specifically, 33% of scientists say they believe in God. For instance, Francis S Collins, Director of the Human Genome Project, the world's largest collaborative biological undertaking, is a scientist and believer and finds no conflict between science, God, and prayer.

Prayer is mentioned very frequently in TDC messages. Once, I was simply told, *"Prayer helps you."*

Many people are alive today, such as the 'high priest of atheism', Richard Dawkins, who scorn prayer and spirituality, favouring answers derived solely from scientific methods. Of course, that is their prerogative, but never forget that scientists once calculated that if a train carriage travelled at more than 21mph, all the air would be sucked out, and the passengers would suffocate.

It is not unusual for people to put God in a box, which allows them to believe that all is well and good with their spiritual lives. Yet, the various tragedies of life have a way of occasionally throwing a wrench into such unrealistic perceptions. Only recently, a very close friend, we have known each other for over fifty years, approached me in a pub where we were having a drink with several other friends; a sort of lad's night out."Can I have a word," he asked, somewhat surreptitiously. I wondered if there was something wrong. And I had good reason.

Five years previously, Anthony had been diagnosed with cancer and had to undergo a rather unpleasant operation. All went well, though, until the cancer returned. He had a second operation, and once again, it appeared everything had gone smoothly; the tumour was gone. However, when he approached me for a 'quiet word', I feared the worst.

I needn't have worried. "I know you know about these kinds of things; in fact, you're the only person I can talk to about this," he began. "Before my first operation five years ago, I reached a real state of despair - I didn't know where to turn or what to do. I remember leaving work and going for a walk to try to clear my head. I know this sounds strange for me, but I ended up sitting in a church (I knew the church well; one of my ancestors is buried there). I was desperate."

Anthony sat silently in a pew near the rear of the church for a few minutes and then did what so many non-believers do in times of great stress and fear. He asked Jesus for help. His petition went something along these lines: "I know I'm not a regular here, and I don't pray or have any particular belief, but if you are up there, I could do with some help. I'm frightened, and I don't know what to do." As he finished what was undoubtedly a prayer - whether he realised it or not - Anthony felt something 'descend' on him, and he suddenly felt elated! "I walked out of the church into the bright sunlight, and I felt great; I knew I was going to be okay."

He needed to 'offload' this experience. He was unsure what to do with it. Still not an overly spiritual person, he was now extremely open-minded, even asking about Christianity. I explained that what had happened to him was pretty common and that he would undoubtedly find his own path as his life progressed. He quite liked this idea, as he said the whole experience had changed him - he had begun to look for something else.

So there I was, standing in the middle of a pub, Guinness in hand, with an old friend, discussing how Jesus had got him through one of the worst days of his life. This, to me, is what Christianity is all about; it's a mystical faith where the supernatural is an everyday event, although very few people understand this. Faith without mysticism is sterility itself. It is just a phantom without life or motion.

It's hard to talk about with the vast majority of folks. Too long has mysticism and paranormal experience been regarded as peculiar, associated with a few strange people. Yet, the thing itself persists. My quest has always been to get to the heart of mysticism, seek out its foundations, discover its fundamental nature, show how it might be practised, and thus ensure it is helpful in our everyday lives.

I have always felt a 'pull' towards mysticism, particularly Christian mysticism (what else would you expect from a monk?), and have always been impressed with the many stories, such as Anthony's, that I've heard. The Gospels record at least thirty-five miracles by Jesus, while the New Testament records many others at the hands of His disciples. Yet, most people claim that we do not experience similar miracles today. I think Anthony would disagree, and so do I.

To put it briefly: The notes on a score are not the music itself, the same way as the words in the Bible and other holy texts are not a direct experience of God's love. Life and experience can only provide that.

Everlasting Pain

"Some things scratch the surface while others strike at your soul."
Gianna Perada

Have you ever been in love? Dreadful, isn't it? It opens up your heart and allows someone else inside, and you have no control over what they will do. I fell in love with my wife despite our differences, and something extraordinary and beautiful was born. For me, love like that has happened just once, and that's why every second we spent together has been imprinted on my soul. The entire universe conspired to help me find her, and, to paraphrase Edgar Allen Poe, I loved with a love that was more than love.

This was unwise on my part. I am a sensitive person, and I knew if I fell in love with Diane, I would be helpless and unprotected if anything happened that was not in the 'script'. Nevertheless, I could feel myself falling from the moment I met her, even though I fought against it for the first year or so. Sensitive people are so vulnerable; they are so easily brutalised and hurt just because they are sensitive. The more sensitive you are, the more confident you can be that at some point, you are going to be brutalised. So although I have put the pieces back together, even though I may look intact, I have never been quite the same as before my wife walked out.

No one had warned me about love's murky underbelly, the rejection and despair, and no one had warned me that the tale of the Fisher King was more than a much-loved myth. And what happened to me on the night of 22 August 2020 was one aspect of this drama that I simply wasn't prepared for. But then horror has quite a penchant for taking one by surprise, and it's hard to be defensive against a danger that you never imagined existed.

It seemed like I was being sentenced to death: "The pain will go on forever." Yet this horrifying message had not been given by a doctor or a hospital consultant; it had arrived via a disembodied voice. This is eternity, it seemed to say, both warning and pleading. For in eternity, there is no time, just a moment long enough to hold unending pain.

The voice was first heard in that strange place between waking and sleeping where reality begins to warp, and it becomes possible to encounter a broad array of sensory experiences, and then as I sat on the edge of the bed, unnerved, completely awake. And it was a voice I recognised: a powerful male voice I had first heard forty-eight years previously.

You may think that madness had come calling, for going mad is sometimes a fitting response to reality. However, this kind of warning voice is not uncommon in parapsychology literature. Kim Penberthy, Professor of Psychiatry and Neurobehavioral Sciences at the University of Virginia, tells the story of a patient who had a terrible alcohol problem. He had tried to stop drinking on many occasions over the years but had consistently failed. However, one day, he arrived at Ms Penberthy's consulting room and cheerfully announced that he had stopped drinking and would never touch a drop again. This announcement was taken with a pinch of salt, as you might expect. Yet months later, he was still dry. When asked how he had achieved this, the man said he had heard a voice while meditating, who he thought 'may' have been his dead mother. She asked him what the hell he was doing and told him to stop drinking because he was killing himself. So he stopped, just like that. Where 21st-century medicine had failed, a disembodied voice had succeeded.

These voices are compelling and persuasive and appear in meditative, hypnagogic (from wakefulness to sleep), and hypnopompic (from sleep to wakefulness) states. It is a phenomenon first described by the Dutch physician Isbrand Van Diemerbroeck in 1664.

I first heard one of these voices back in 1972 when, as a fifteen-year-old boy, I stayed overnight in a house my parents had bought but had yet to decorate or furnish. Consequently, there was just me, a single bed, a kettle, and a mug. Aside from that, the place was utterly deserted. I was sleeping there because, on Saturday mornings, I used to play in a football team, and the new house was far more convenient for meeting up with my teammates.

On one particular Saturday morning, at around 7.45 am, I was lying wide awake in bed, trying to draw the energy together to get up. I had to be out of the door at 9.00 am. Suddenly, I heard a thunderous, compelling masculine voice shout, "Rod!" I sprang up and sat on the edge of the bed, trying to get my thoughts together. Then again, "Rod!" The monsters, it seemed, were no longer living in my closet or under my bed.

It wasn't until that evening that I discovered why the voice had materialised. It was a warning. My father had found that my mother was having an affair, kicking off years of recriminations and appalling arguments. Now, in August 2020, the voice had returned, and I recognised it instantly. It was another warning – know that there is always a price to pay for unconditional love.

My life had been spiralling out of control for approximately eighteen months, and my marriage was in trouble. There were no third parties or abuse of any kind involved. We still loved each other, but some external issues had arisen. The fact is that we were no longer heavenly angels, more like prison inmates with wings. It is unnecessary to explain the actual reasons for the separation, just the fallout and the psychic kickback I am experiencing as a result. It wasn't just confined to the claim that 'the pain will go on forever', either, as we will discover.

When the break-up first occurred, I freely admit that I did not cope well at all. When Diane first announced that she was leaving, I must have looked at her the same way Julius Caesar looked at Brutus.

I unravelled very quickly, and within days had got to the point where I no longer wanted to live and was actively looking for a way out. I couldn't eat, and I couldn't sleep. I suffered from nearly every symptom that can be associated with anxiety and depression, from numbness, dizziness, chest pain, and nausea through to heart palpitations, panic attacks, and a choking feeling in my throat. All I felt were fear and pain. I lost over a stone-and-a-half in weight. I was not doing well in terms of being a functional human being.

My wife walked out on a Saturday evening and, by the following Friday, I was disoriented and bewildered. I didn't want to die, but the pain was so great that I felt I could no longer go on living. It's important to remember, too, that I didn't just lose my wife; I lost an entire family, including my four-year-old granddaughter, who I loved to bits. All of this occurred during lockdown, so isolation had also taken a firm grip on my mind.

I felt as cut off as a hermit in a cave in the middle of the Sinai Desert. In reality, I was in a house with a bay window as my only visual interface with the world. It took me two days to fully realise that I was not going to be able to see anyone at all. And, to mix my metaphors, there I was, alone in my urban jungle, like a caged tiger.

At this time, I came to understand that the opposite of love is not hate; it is loneliness. Open a dictionary and look up loneliness. You will see a definition such as 'being without company, cut off from others, sadness from being alone, producing a feeling of bleakness or desolation', all of which is true. It is not the entire story, though. There is another level of loneliness, which I shall term 'spiritual loneliness'. This has nothing to do with everyday Earthly loneliness; it is not 'the blues' or even depression. It is something 'other'; it is from someplace else; it's an abyss, a void. It is love's hideous and macabre twin brother and can put you in a strange place, a place where, in this life, you are probably not supposed to go.

I have been lucky, enjoying many psychic and mystical experiences – I am a believer in the sacred and the sanctity of the human soul. Yet, experiencing spiritual loneliness can make life intolerable and seemingly pointless. It can make you want to consent to a death sentence without a whimper simply to break away from the life sentence that destiny holds in her other hand.

It is essential to appreciate that although the immediate danger of ending one's life and 'returning home' may pass, the underlying reason is still there. It's like a dandelion. You pull up the flower, oblivious to the fact that the roots are extensive and deep. You survive, but the call of the abyss never entirely goes away. But you learn not to answer it.

The emotional and spiritual pain, though, is excruciating. For if love is genuine, it never dies, but transforms itself from the most beautiful thing on Earth to the most nightmarish and dreadful emotion anyone could imagine.

Did I pray? You bet your sweet bippy I did! But there was no answer; no one was there to sort out my problem, to put everything right, which was, in fact, what I was asking God for. And then I remembered that when Jesus was in the Garden of Gethsemane, before being arrested, he prayed, imploring, "Father, if you are willing, take this cup away from me." He didn't. So I knew He sure as hell wasn't going to take my 'cup' away!

Many Christians are unsettled by Jesus' appeal to have the cup taken from him. Didn't he come to die, after all? Wasn't this his mission? I can't begin to answer these questions in any meaningful way. But what I see in Jesus' prayer is a real human being, fully human and fully divine. I snatch a brief look at the indescribable horror that awaits him. I see a Jesus to whom I can relate, one who is much more like me than the superman Jesus who goes to the cross without a second thought and little hesitation.

My 'cup' may not be on the scale of His, but it is still, for me, too awful for words. However, while God did not sort out my crisis, I did feel supported on many occasions when my head was dipping below the waves. And I knew that being shown mercy in these instances meant that 'someone' was close – and it required a line to be drawn in the sand for that 'someone' to stand up for the 'accused'. Someone was on my side.

The Amfortas Wound

"One thing you can't hide - is when you're crippled inside."
  John Lennon

Life challenges are not merely indiscriminate, arbitrary, or meaningless, and a more profound appreciation of life's possibilities takes hold when you understand that you designed your own life path - before you were even born. The relationships you encounter and the challenges you confront, you planned them out in detail so you could develop as a soul. Still, even knowing this, it is sometimes difficult to answer some of the more taxing questions about your incarnation

For me, the most pressing question is whether the suffering will continue indefinitely. So far, more than a year after the break-up, the answer is a resounding yes. I have discovered that the pain I am experiencing is like water; it finds its way through any seal. There's no way to stop it. As a result, the disembodied voice that proclaimed, "The pain will go on forever", was correct.

There are precedents for this kind of everlasting pain, too, most notably in literature in the tale of medieval knights whose lifelong quest it was to recover the Holy Grail – the cup that Jesus drank from at the Last Supper. I mention this because a couple of years before the separation, my wife, who follows the shamanic path, took me on a shamanic journey, guiding me into an altered state of consciousness. While in that state, I was aware of and very clearly heard the name 'Gawain'.

Sir Gawain was King Arthur's nephew and a Knight of the Round Table in Arthurian Legend. In the earliest

Arthurian literature, he appeared as a model of knightly perfection, against whom all other knights were measured. He was also a Grail Knight.

The Grail story is one of the world's great legends and includes the tale of the Fisher King, Amfortas, also known as the Wounded King. There are several versions about what happened to Amfortas, from being burned in the groin by a salmon he was cooking to being castrated by a pagan knight, but all agree on one thing, the painful wound would not heal. Amfortas arrives at the Holy Lake at one stage, borne on a stretcher by Knights of the Grail. He calls out for Gawain, whose attempt at relieving his pain had failed. But Gawain had already left, seeking a new remedy.

There is, of course, much more to this story, but for me, the fact that I was taken on a journey where I recognised Gawain, and then finding this linked to the Fisher King, whose wound wouldn't heal, whose pain would go on forever, was enough to give me pause for thought. Then there was the fact that Gawain had tried to relieve Amfortas's pain but had failed. It was apt, too, that my wife guided me on this journey – giving me a foretaste of what was to come. For she was to become the 'pagan knight'.

In Richard Wagner's last opera, Parsifal, Amfortas determined that it was his duty to destroy the power of the evil Klingsor, who threatened the Holy Grail. He journeyed to Klingsor's castle, armed with the Holy Spear, which pierced Christ's side on the Cross. But he fell under the spell of Kundry, and while she seduced him, Klingsor stole the Spear and used it to pierce Amfortas. His wound will not heal, and Amfortas is in relentless agony.

Several recent TDC messages I have received talk of a castle. These include *"You go up into the castle"* and *"You leave her now in the castle."* Klingsor's castle had now, it seemed, been added to the Gawain incident I had with Diane to underline the reality of the 'Amfortas Wound' – Spirit was starting to guide me through this whole experience using mythology. It was a mythology that they knew I would understand, too, as Parsifal is one of my favourite operas.

Yet, why am I given insights into my current predicament? Why doesn't it just play out? I have a few ideas about this; not least, I have a degree of support because I am being put through something that I am not well equipped to cope with. Indeed, on one occasion, I was told through TDC that *"Roderick, you can't live with all the pain."*

The Darkness

"To fight evil, you have to understand the dark."
Nalini Singh, Heart of Obsidian

I did not begin when I was born, nor when I was conceived. That is at the heart of my credo. I know that I started loving Diane before this present incarnation, and it feels like a commitment to eternity I made a long time ago.

Within the concept of reincarnation, karma is unfinished spiritual business. On the level of the soul, it's your to-do list. However, like gravity, karma is so fundamental we rarely notice it. In the modern world, an ever-growing number of people say they believe in karma when, in fact, they believe in revenge. But at the core of karma is one straightforward rule – how you treat others is how karma treats you.

It is said that most people have some sort of karmic relationship with at least one other person. Adherents of reincarnation believe that before we incarnate, we create a soul contract in which we make agreements to heal past life karmic relationships. I can imagine, prior to birth, my wife saying to me, "This is going to hurt me a lot more than it hurts you." Of course, like the parent who tells the child the same thing, the truth would be a little different.

The law of karma is an unbending and impersonal rule of the universe, and it is once again attracting the minds of both intellectuals and the general public. Films, novels, popular songs, and periodicals now incorporate reincarnation with ever-increasing frequency. Millions of Westerners are rapidly joining ranks with more than 1.5 billion people, including Hindus, Buddhists, Taoists, and members of other faiths, including followers of early Christianity. These are people who have traditionally understood that life does not begin at birth nor end with death.

Sometimes, lives get crossed; memories appear that do not belong in this incarnation; feelings rise to the surface that are too powerful to control. Moreover, sometimes we get warnings about events way in advance. In my case, it came through a rather dark peak experience.

No, peak experiences are not always pleasant. In March of 1983, a little less than two months after the beautiful mystical experience where I was engulfed with 'spiritual electricity' for eight hours, the 'electrical energy' returned. I was sitting talking to Catherine, with who I had enjoyed the previous encounter. We were in the same room as before, and this time we were joined by Catherine's younger sister, Josie. The discussion was centred on that January night when Catherine and I were in the presence of something truly amazing and otherworldly. Then the atmosphere changed.

The room became silent – and aware. Suddenly, I realised what this was about, and I explained what I was feeling. "It's about loneliness." As I spoke, I felt something very real turn in my stomach, and a feeling so desolate, forbidding, and wretched came over me that I was frozen to the spot. This feeling only lasted for around ten seconds, but it was genuinely terrifying. There was a total void, a complete lack of anything, except utter loneliness.

At the same time as this was happening, Catherine and Josie burst into floods of uncontrollable tears. I have never seen two people so disturbed, but again this lasted only for around ten seconds, then they wiped their eyes and started to discuss what we had all just experienced. It was all very strange, like we had slipped out of everyday existence for a matter of seconds into what can only be described as an abyss. Unfortunately, just over thirty-seven years later, it would return, and this time it would do enormous mental and emotional damage, underlined by the statement, "The pain will go on forever."

I did not realise back then that this experience, which came and went so quickly, was a forewarning of spiritual repercussions that would shake my life to its foundations. As the years went on, I did begin to have clues that something was out of kilter. Some of these came through TDC, with messages given in response to questions about reincarnation and karma, such as, *"You are in peril now."* I don't suppose many people consider 'peril' when they talk about karma, but I guess it's obvious when you think about it. Today, karma has almost entered the realm of fluffy bunnies for most people, but it can and does become vicious, cruel, and almost sadistic. It's a learning curve, but what a learning curve, particularly as you don't know what you're supposed to be learning!

I recall one very clear TDC I received that was, in retrospect, a sign that this incarnation is being held in a classroom with a very stern teacher who possesses a cane that can draw blood: *"Enough now, almost given his punishment."* The word 'almost' struck home when I first listened to this message; there was more to come. I now know what that 'more' is, and I don't think I was looking forward to it in a soul sense. On another occasion, when discussing past lives with a friend, I picked up my own soul, which uttered the immortal words, *"Coming down to the Earth on this damn bloody rock!"* I clearly wasn't keen on having another physical life, and I was now beginning to understand why.

When I tell people about this and start to discuss karmic retribution, one question invariably crops up: is there is a cosmic evil or darkness? The answer is yes, and anyone with an open mind can see that this is the case in the world today: war, greed, murder, animal cruelty, racism - the list is practically endless. Just because someone dies and moves onto another plane, it does not make them instantly angelic. We are all at different stages of spiritual evolution, and if Earth is a school, it is no more advanced than a kindergarten.

What's more, and this is extremely important for all those with a spiritual practice, your state of mind will determine which realm or type of spirits you attract. This was brought home to me during Brexit, the national commitment to self-harm recently witnessed in the UK. Now, excuse me for being mildly political at this juncture; this is important. Think of it as spiritual health and safety, if you will.

I usually possess a reasonably good state of spiritual equilibrium. I try not to let the shenanigans of politicians and money-grabbing business people get to me. This has allowed me to communicate with a wide array of spiritual beings, several of which I have known on this Earth. However, during Brexit, I began to feel angry with both British politicians and the general populace. In truth, I had become ashamed to be British. Feeling this level of anger is not acceptable on any level, but spiritually it can be particularly problematic.

Throughout much of this rather dark period, I found that I was regularly attracting very unpleasant entities whenever I contacted Spirit. They were not necessarily dangerous, but they were crude, threatening, and obnoxious. Moreover, I couldn't get past them to the higher planes. I was 'vibrating', to use old terminology, at a slower rate, which stopped me from 'reaching up towards the light'.

If people think dark thoughts - hatred, racism, intolerance, revenge, etc. - it will impact the 'health' of their soul, and for those with a link to Spirit, it is a crystal clear invitation to the 'dark side of the force'. I have experienced this. It is not good.

It is essential to realise that in the physical world, darkness is passive. It exists wherever light is absent. Wherever light shines, darkness is instantly eradicated. This is not so with spiritual darkness. Spiritual darkness is not passive but active. Most adults will tell you that almost every child in the world has an irrational fear of the dark. But it's not irrational.

TDC supports this point of view. When I inquired about the topic of evil and how karma was affecting my current life, the response was, *"You will face a lot of spirits."* These spirits can affect the people around you, too; normally kind people can become cruel; honest people start to lie; happy people become sad. Although their attitude to life can invite the darkness in, the people themselves are often not wholly to blame. Regardless of that, they are fed thoughts and ideas from what TDC calls 'the darkness' and what Eastern Orthodox Christians call logismoi. I received one TDC message that suggested that this was indeed the case when I asked why my wife had suddenly turned on me: *"Just love her, Rod; someone's tricked you."*

Logismoi, or the darkness, are thought-forms placed into people's heads by unhelpful spirits or what people call demons. The darkness can stop us from reaching God; that's the point of it.

These negative entities have assaulted me, but instead of the darkness being fed directly into my head, they have appeared as verbal attacks on my computer. The following is an excellent example of how these unpleasant spirits work: *"Rod, you love a woman called Diane ... she's on the phone now ... she's going out with a gentleman from*

Derby ... she's spoken with Alan ... they are talking right now."

These, of course, are the sort of thoughts many people have when they split with their partner. Where are they? Who are they with? Have they found someone else? More often than not, though, these thoughts have been whispered by the darkness; they are not the original thoughts of the person having them. With TDC, it is easy to see how this all works.

I am fortunate that I have friends and guides in Spirit who tell me what's happening. Consequently, seconds after the 'your wife is having an affair with Alan, a guy from Derby' suggestion, I received another string of messages to straighten things out: *"They are messing with you Rod, they're testing you ... bad people ... Roderick, they are lying."*

If that second set of messages hadn't come through, I would probably have started imagining all sorts of stuff. That's the way the darkness works – you know the idea is probably nonsense, but you can't get it out of your head. They are spiritual earworms.

The darkness is an outside influence and a little like receiving a threatening, although enticing, letter. The inner spiritual world becomes contaminated, and you are affected on a profound level, sometimes leaving you feeling helpless. For the darkness does not only taunt you. It also makes suggestions. The desire to commit adultery is an excellent example. The potential adulterous relationship does not make sense on any level (apart from simple lust), but many people can't help themselves. And interestingly, when they do manage to pull away, the problem often only gets worse, and the next time they see the object of their affection, the noose tightens.

Nowadays, in the face of the darkness, I say, "Is that the best you can do?" I don't say this to start a fight, but to let them know that my faith, strength, and protection are far greater than theirs, that I cannot be taken away from my own sacred path by their attacks and silly behaviour. I ask them this question whenever I'm blocked, and it's given me the courage to keep going.

Most Christians will tell you that it is wrong to communicate with demons, even if it is to tell them to go away. Only the holy and exorcists should ever attempt such a thing, they argue. But in Mark 9:38-39, it says: "Teacher," said John, "we saw someone driving out demons in your name, and we told him to stop because he was not one of us." "Do not stop him," Jesus said. "For no one who does a miracle in my name can in the next moment say anything bad about me."

Jesus knew that the power to dispel demons was not in who you knew but what you knew; if you had genuine faith and trust in God, you were protected and had the power to perform mighty deeds. Today, the Church mostly ignores the demonic or the darkness, but it is real, and it is active.

Nevertheless, most people are not even aware of this form of malevolence, and those worst affected tend to have troubled lives; it just seems like one problem after another. But in our 'enlightened' times, most of those affected do not even consider the possibility of the darkness – even those who do tend to ignore it. Taking action requires you to take responsibility for your life and change (what is known as metanoia – a complete change of heart), for it is so much easier for the darkness to operate with those who are not leading the lives they should be.

Rudolf Steiner, one of the world's most prolific and gifted scientists and philosophers, devoted much of his work to the task of peering beyond 'the veil', sharing his insight into the deeper nature of life and of the world beyond.

On the topic of anxiety and depression, Steiner spoke of hostile beings in the spiritual world that influence and feed off human emotion. This belief also holds true for shamans and others who access the spiritual dimensions to alleviate their patients' mental suffering.

Many are familiar with the idea of energy vampires or people who suck your energy and feed off your negative emotions. On the existence of similar entities in other dimensions, Steiner wrote: "There are beings in the spiritual realms for whom anxiety and fear emanating from human beings offer welcome food. When humans have no anxiety and fear, then these creatures starve. People not yet sufficiently convinced of this statement could understand it to be meant comparatively only. But for those who are familiar with this phenomenon, it is a reality. If fear and anxiety radiates from people, and they break out in panic, then these creatures find welcome nutrition, and they become more and more powerful. These beings are hostile towards humanity.

"Everything that feeds on negative feelings, on anxiety, fear and superstition, despair or doubt, are in reality hostile forces in super-sensible worlds, launching cruel attacks on human beings, while they are being fed. Therefore, it is, above all, necessary that the person who enters the spiritual world overcomes fear, feelings of helplessness, despair, and anxiety. But these are exactly the feelings that belong to contemporary culture and materialism; because it estranges people from the spiritual world, it is especially suited to evoke hopelessness and fear of the unknown in people, thereby calling up the above mentioned hostile forces against them."

In today's world, which has worked hard to eradicate traditional philosophical understanding, an idea like

Steiner's is not readily accepted. Bernhard Guenther, renowned for his study and practice in yoga, qi gong, meditation, dance, psychology, and shamanism, has this to say on the subject: "And yet, despite the cynical scepticism, all of the ancient mystery schools, true shamanic insights, and esoteric teachings (much of which have been suppressed or distorted over thousands of years for obvious reasons) have conveyed this truth for 'the ones with eyes to see and ears to hear', using their own language and symbolism, be it The General Law (Esoteric Christianity), Archons (Gnostics), Lords of Destiny (Hermeticism), Predator/Fliers (Shamanism, Castaneda), The Evil Magician (Gurdjieff), The Shaitans (Sufism), The Jinn (Arabian mythology), Wetiko (Native American Spirituality), Occult Hostile Forces (Sri Aurobindo and The Mother) etc."

I once picked up a TDC message where these spirits confessed to what they were doing: *"I mess with their thoughts."*

Of course, this does not absolve us of all responsibility for what we say or do. Quite the opposite. It is usually people with a disturbing side to their nature that the darkness is most attracted to. One woman, for instance, clearly stated through TDC, *"I am going to lie."* She did. But mark my words, she'll get what's coming to her, not only because of the darkness, but because karma is a bigger bitch than she is!

Strangely, many people who attract this darkness to the degree that it starts to destroy the lives of everyone around them (and eventually their own) are wildly popular – their friends and family think they are close to sainthood. Many years ago, I had a friend who fitted this description perfectly, although, at the time, I knew nothing of the darkness.

Mark was a wheeler-dealer, into everything but doing very little. Worse still, he was married to a good friend of mine, Vicky, and he was cheating on her, over and over again. I knew this was going on - he even introduced me to two of his lovers, and I did nothing. It's something I am ashamed of to this day. Having said that, I did eventually snap. He was taking one of his lady friends on a weekend away, pretending to be on a business trip, and because of this, he was going to miss Vicky's birthday. When he returned, though, he had bought a gift for his wife ... a Mars Bar.

That was it. I told her everything. She didn't believe me. Neither did any of her brothers and sisters. I never saw her again.

Mark was calculating and arrogant. Yet, everyone loved him and believed everything he said. But it wasn't just this that made him stand out as being manipulated by the darkness, which, as one psychic medium said to me, tends to wrap itself around its victim like a serpent. For when the darkness is present, strange little psychic happenings can occur. And often, they derive from those closest to the person in question, not themselves. The serpent appears to be reaching out to claim yet another victim.

In the case of Mark, it was his young son, Zach. A lively four-year-old, he had once surprised us while we were sitting in the garden by turning very serious for a moment, looking straight at me, and proclaiming, "A dove has just flown out of the top of your head." His mom wasn't even sure where he'd got the word 'dove' from. But kids are a little psychic at that age; some of them even remember past lives. What they cannot do is remote viewing.

I had arrived at Mark and Vicky's house one sunny summer afternoon, having just purchased a new car (but hadn't picked it up yet), which I announced as we sat down to enjoy a drink in the garden. Upon hearing this, Zach asked, "Is that the red one, like Uncle Terry's?" The car I had bought was indeed red and, it turned out, was the same make as Uncle Terry's. How could a four-year-old know this? He couldn't have unless 'something' told him. People tend to think this kind of thing is 'cute' – it isn't. Knowledge of the unknowable in such circumstances is the quickest test of infestation by the darkness. Those witnessing such things need to ask themselves how it is even possible and not just giggle about it, which is the usual response to anything people do not understand in modern Britain. It's a flag. A bloody big red one!

I have known others with the same malaise as Mark, and if you know what to look for, the darkness is easy to spot. The problem *can be* relatively easy to 'cure' too. Yet, helping people affected this way can be one challenge too many because friends and family surround them like wagons on the prairie. They can do no wrong. The darkness is clever; it is preternatural and has played this game for a long time.

Winter Snow

"Oh deep winter snow, pale executioner, thou who delights in a slow, torturous death."
T. R. Neff, The Falconer and The Wolf

What had I done in a previous life to deserve such karmic wrath? It is important to remember that this was not just the heartbreak of losing my wife. It was the fact that the 'abyss' I experienced in 1983 came back thirty-seven years later, on the day she walked out. I decided to question the spirit world. Now, I realise that to many people, the idea of asking Spirit questions via a computer and getting answers back in real-time is ludicrous. I have to say I couldn't agree more. But it happens - all the time.

In the initial session, explicitly asking for information on the life that is causing a karmic rebound in this one, I was first told, *"Roderick was born with me in Sicily ... didn't it get cold?"* This last reference brings up the idea of snow and winter, which Pauline mentioned when she wrote down the list of words, names, and phrases linked to Sicily.

Winter is like unrequited love, freezing and pitiless. Over the past couple of years, winter and snow have repeatedly been mentioned in TDC messages. Some of these I didn't understand at the time, such as *"Snow in May."* This message was given in November 2019 – my wife left in May 2020. I also found a couple of voices riding off the back of Diane speaking, both recorded in January 2020: *"Remember this last time, and it snowed"* and *"Sorry, it snowed."*

Is it just a coincidence, too, that during our honeymoon in Venice, it snowed? We were having a lovely lunch in

Trattoria Ai Cugnai near the Ponte dell' Accademia when it began – one of the most romantic cities on Earth suddenly became even more so. It was magical. But, could it have been an omen, even a message at some deep level considering the above TDC statements spoken by Diane? How far down the rabbit hole do you want to go?

Since the separation, I have received many voices related to winter, including *"Listen, it's winter now"* and *"It's so cold in winter."* Another string of messages, this time in April 2019, proclaimed: *"We shall speak about winter ... it's going to be cold ... top of the day, but the future is real rough."*

The future was rough, yet I still hoped that there would be a thaw of the winter in 2021, that Diane would at least acknowledge my existence. I thought that by March, the snow would melt a little. But not that year. Day after day, the frost stayed hard; the world remained hostile and remote. Winter, like me, appeared to be exhausted; it dropped to its knees and waited. What it was waiting for, I am still not sure. Diane was the most beautiful thing I had ever seen, a wounded angel in the snow, but she was gone. What was I waiting for?

And throughout all this, the Sicily experience remained. Something had happened back in the 17th-century, and it had probably occurred in the snow. Most people seem to think of the island as a sun-kissed paradise yet forget that it has ski resorts and that its high peaks, including Mount Etna, are covered in snow for several months of the year. I am convinced that there is a link with Sicily, the winter dreams and messages, and my failed marriage.

This assumption was backed up by a psychic medium in early 2021 who mentioned this particular past life: "You brought a past life into this life – a difficult life; it was in the 1600s, and you wouldn't have been able to do what you wanted to do, and you would have known hardship, it was cold and unforgiving. But you learned to be on your own in that life. In this lifetime, you try to escape any form of imprisonment."

That is very true. One of my favourite songs, Bird on a Wire, has the lyric: 'Like a bird on a wire, like a drunk in a midnight choir, I have tried in my way to be free'. Those are words that always send a tingle down my spine.

So it appears that the Sicilian past is wreaking havoc in this one. I don't yet understand, though, why Diane has acted the way she has, with so little compassion, something that is entirely out of character. *"Diane has been hard with you, hasn't she?"* one TDC voice said. Yes, she has, and it makes coping with this situation so much more difficult, but perhaps that's the point.

It's important to say at this stage that the spirit communicators do not just come through with statements and answers to questions; on occasion, they also intervene. In one instance, towards the end of November 2020, they could well have saved my life. It was around 9.00 pm on a Monday, and I was missing my wife terribly. As the voice had told me, the pain will go on forever – it is constant, it never leaves me for a second. Nevertheless, there are times when this pain was joined by the solitude and loneliness of lockdown and the silence of a winter's night, and on this occasion, I became wrapped in a cocoon of anguish.

My mind drifted to the idea of death and how comforting it would be not to feel the pain – what a relief that would be. Then something extraordinary occurred.

I have always had a passion for cats; for me, one of God's most beautiful, graceful, and intelligent creatures. Several years ago, I had heard about one of my feline friends through TDC who had passed over in 1994: *"Shady with grandma."* This statement made sense to me;

Shady, my cat, was with my mother, who, when she saw her, always said: "Come and see your grandma." Even so, the following TDC communication was beyond my wildest dreams.

A voice appeared saying, *"Shady ... the cat ... look what it did, your cat ... she's over there."* Then the message continued, from Shady herself*, "I'm forty ... you go on without me ... we are all here, we're purring ... we're waiting for you ... I am a tortoiseshell."*

If cats lived to that kind of age, Shady would indeed have been forty in 2020, and she was a tortoiseshell. Getting this message through lifted my spirits no end; the idea that all of my cats were waiting for me, purring, was the stuff of dreams. On the other side, my friends knew that I was getting close to a very bad place and arranged something special to pull me out.

Around this time, I also discovered that my subconscious/soul understands Italian, a language I would love to learn, but, well, I'm rubbish with learning new languages. This revelation resulted from a dream where I was listening to the Italian song 'Volare'. I couldn't understand why this song would come into my head, whether asleep or awake, but upon translating the lyrics into English, it quickly became apparent.

On more than one occasion, I have told Diane that she is 'my dream', and on the evening before hearing the song while fast asleep, I had been thinking about this; about all of the things that add up to her being my dream. The very first line of Volare is: 'I think a similar dream will never come back'.

Did I receive a message in Italian in my sleep because I was once a Sicilian monk? Or maybe it was because we all have this facility to understand other languages when 'detached' from our everyday consciousness? I like to think it's the latter.

105

On one occasion, Spirit even sent me a gift! This was before the separation, but at the time, I felt extremely low. I now understand that I had been badly depressed for three or four years before my wife left. We had not been allowed to get on with our lives; the feeling had become claustrophobic, and I felt constantly despondent. At this time, I was a member of Audible, Amazon's audiobook division. One evening, I went into Audible to listen to a book I had downloaded and to my astonishment, there was another book at the top of the list - 'A Call from Heaven: Personal Accounts of Deathbed Visits, Angelic Visions, and Crossings to the Other Side' by Josie Varga.

I know I didn't order it, and upon a bit of investigation, I discovered that I didn't pay for it either. So via TDC, I asked about this, and the reply was, *"Rod, the Call was fantastic!"* This message came out of total silence, and they were clearly pleased with themselves. Again, though, I appreciated the concern and the love that came with it.

The spiritual world is full of surprises. On another occasion, I had recorded a conversation between my wife, step-daughter, and myself about past lives. I started to say (via TDC), *"I was in love with you,"* but I was cut off by both women declaring, *"Oh, shut up, we know who you are!"* Two souls were speaking in unison.

I certainly knew them both in the between-life state, too, with Spirit underlining this many times, including, *"Do you remember Mandy over here?"* And strangely, I kind of do remember my step-daughter, which I guess is why they asked. Just six months before the separation with my wife, I recorded Mandy when we talked about the future, saying, via TDC, *"Scared for him, I'm screaming."* I believe that she knew what would happen on a soul level and was fearful of the whole idea. Unfortunately, that has not translated into any kind of empathy in the current situation.

Therefore, it is good that a year after the separation with Diane, I do not miss or think about Mandy. I used to care a lot for her, but that feeling has faded. Yet over the past six months, she has started to pop up in my dreams as a friend, a confidante, someone who knows me at a deep level. And the morning after I have these dreams, I feel very close to her again for just an hour or two. It's the strangest feeling.

I questioned Spirit about this and received an interesting but baffling response: *"Mandy was there ... don't forget it ... and you promised her ... is that clear?"* Mandy had already told me via TDC over a year before that, *"You're standing in for me; it's an old promise."* So this second mention of a 'promise' is intriguing.

A Karmic Calamity

"Dear Karma, I really hate you right now; you made your point."
  Ottilie Weber, Family Ties

The treachery of demons pales in comparison to an angel's betrayal. Diane betrayed our trust, our love, and our friendship. But if she thinks that my love for her is so feeble that betraying me would make a difference, she simply doesn't know me.

Perhaps she thought cutting me off was a kindness; that I would be able to forget her and get on with life. In the real world, though, when we're talking about unconditional love and the Amfortas Wound, it simply doesn't work. It might work with a teenage crush, but not with me.

Forget the 'bump in the night' stuff; it's loss that does it for me. Karma is a cruel harlot; of that, there is no doubt, but I would say "I love you" with my last breath if I had to choose between breathing and loving Diane. Sweet, eh? No, not really. It is a karmic calamity – and it is going on forever.

Yet, sometimes something new and strange occurs, something that tries to lift me, something that tries to let me know that I am not on my own, such as when a different aspect of myself came calling. I'm still trying to wrap my head around the implications, but in early December 2020, the following very long string of messages came through: *"Rod, we have Philip with us,"* which was followed by a few seconds of static, and then *"I want to talk with you ... you've found the monk ... what happened with Diane is very wrong ... helping with you on that ... you are different ... I am Philip ... Roderick, I am the monk ... you must start working ... you have a purpose ... I am alive in you ... you are part of me ... I am not reflected."*

I asked if that means the monk is actually an aspect of me, and the messages continued: *"I am ... I am Philip ... I am you ... I must keep working ... if I come and work with you, you won't be on your own ... only that woman will help you."* The voices then changed, and I realised immediately that the darkness was back. I prayed, and before the recording came to an end, I received the following message: *"I am Philip ... you are crying ... they know that."*

I think what had happened here was that when I was told "only that woman will help you", my thoughts went immediately to Diane, and I felt fear, fear that I would never see her again. Also, fear that the only cure for the Fisher King came in the form of that which had wounded him. For me, that meant Diane, and that seemed highly unlikely. The darkness picked up this fear and, although I wasn't physically crying, I understood the inference.

Following these messages, I began to wonder whether there were two monks (a guide and myself) or just my higher self. So I asked. *"You are a monk ... you have faith ... you're watching the family."* Not a very straightforward answer: in fact, not an answer at all. But this is what sometimes happens with TDC; they don't always tell you what you want to know, but what they want, or need, to say to you. Sometimes they are almost like Zen koans – puzzles wrapped in an enigma. The following string of messages illustrates this; it was recorded the day after my birthday in December 2020: *"Rod, you must see the process ... Diane, it must have been rough; you're shattered ... I'm watching you, Rod ... you've been with us for centuries, Rod ... I've seen our monks get burned ... in the forest, you're surrounded ... send for the guide that's helping you ... help you to rest, it will be bad, it's true. "*

Life is both happy and distressing, yin and yang, and as Buddha rightly states, there is no escaping pain in this world. That's why, at various points in our journey, we have to confront the shadow side of existence. Shamanic traditions worldwide tell us that the Hero's Journey involves dismemberment and pain but that this experience ultimately results in re-birth and greater wisdom. Or, as Oprah Winfrey once said, "Turn your wounds into wisdom." This is my aim.

But I do feel that there are two monks, one a guide and one myself. Whatever is happening, I have changed. I am now someone who lives a different life from most people, although the intensity of the pain never diminishes, even for one second. Nevertheless, I feel blessed because I lead an intriguing life and always have done. But most of all, I feel blessed because I communicate daily with Spirit and have achieved unconditional love. I have had to start to 'own' who and what I am.

Sailing off the Coast of Sunderland

"Love is a violent recreational sport. Proceed at your own risk. Helmets, armour, and steel-toe boots are required by law."
  H.C. Paye

In life, everyone suffers and makes mistakes. It's the same with Spirit, and it is crucial to be discerning. Those who ignore this simple dictum can get into all sorts of trouble.

The River Trent, close to where I live, is beautiful. It is light, dancing, rippling, and sparkling. But there is always darkness, always something lurking. This is true of the spirit world – there is good and evil, light and dark. It can be scary sometimes.

Only recently, I was verbally 'picked on' in a spiritual sense; they were trying to frighten me. My guide intervened to tell me, *"You are being attacked."* I asked why I was being attacked, and my guide responded, *"You are human, you are a monk, you have the power."*

The dark spirits do not like humans, but they also don't like the fact that spiritually speaking, I have specific knowledge and abilities that have been carried over from former incarnations. This is why I can do what I do, I believe. Regarding 'the power', this is simply a term used by many psychic mediums to explain what they are utilising when they are in touch with Spirit.

My monk guide can be quite forthcoming. I once asked him if he had been with me since birth, and he replied, *"I'll tell you something; you're in my family, Roderick."* I suggested that being my guide must be a challenging assignment. He responded somewhat enigmatically by saying, *"Roderick, I am electric."* I asked if that was why I felt electricity/strong tingles when he was close, and he said, *"I have blended with you; I am blending now with you."* He also explained that he has to slowly get the hang of communicating through a computer, *"I'm learning, Roderick, to communicate."*

Sometimes I have wanted to ask my guide, "Why didn't you tell me love hurt this freaking much?" Of course, once we're in that 'raft', lost at sea, we keep hoping for a shift in the wind, hoping that we'll soon be cruising off the coast of Santorini, where the waters are calm. However, we invariably seem to drift closer to Sunderland than Santorini.

Let me illustrate.

If you have ever been deeply in love with someone, you may have described the close connection you had as being on the level of 'soul mates'. This means much more than just being suited to one another or having an overwhelming attraction. Instead, it is a spiritual connection that you feel, well, spiritually. But what does this mean? It's a feeling that you cannot begin to explain, even to yourself. You just know that you belong with this person. Yet, there is a dark twist to this most profound state of love, and it can quite literally kill you.

For instance, Mary Tamm was a British actress perhaps best remembered for her role as Romana in the BBC's science fiction series Doctor Who in the late 1970s. On 26 July 2012, she died after a long battle with cancer. Marcus Ringrose, her husband of thirty-four years, died just hours after delivering the eulogy at his wife's funeral while sitting writing thank you notes to those who had sent their condolences. Cases such as these are not infrequent.

A broken heart can squeeze the life out of you; it can crush you like a bug. When you're in a long-term relationship and that 'soul mate' thing is in play, heartbreak can bring your entire world to an end. Your soul is damaged, a large wound appears that you can feel, but it cannot be seen, and it is impossible to explain how it feels. But unlike 'run-of-the-mill' broken hearts, it does not get better with time; the pain goes on and on.

Perhaps it's a testimony to the power of love. Couples can feel so intensely that when one spouse dies, the other succumbs soon after. However, it is not only death that can cause this kind of unimaginable pain. It can also be caused by separation and divorce. Separating from my wife was the most crushing event of my life. Yet it wasn't textbook, at least not a medical or psychological textbook. It had a huge spiritual element, which first began to work loose decades before I met Diane. In retrospect, it looks like the whole thing was planned, sort of a pre-life contract. That does not make it any easier. In some ways, it makes it worse.

And, of course, there was still the physical backlash to cope with – in my case, 'broken heart syndrome', known more formally as 'takotsubo cardiomyopathy'. This is usually a temporary condition where the heart muscle becomes suddenly weakened or stunned, and the left ventricle, one of the heart's chambers, changes shape. This stops the heart from pumping correctly and reduces blood flow out of the heart.

It can feel like a heart attack – mine was also accompanied by chest pains, breathlessness, and nausea – but it is not a heart attack. A heart attack occurs because of a blockage in an artery, usually due to coronary artery disease. During a takotsubo event, there is no blockage in the arteries. Instead, there is a temporary 'stunning' of the heart muscle. It is a very unpleasant experience, but happily, the chance of having a second one is relatively low.

For some people, those sick or close to the end of their lives, 'broken heart syndrome' can be bitter-sweet. Naturally, there is the grief of the bereaved family who has lost two people they love. However, there is frequently a sense of relief that two individuals who were so much in love have crossed over together.

Don and Maxine Simpson, from Bakersfield, California, died just four hours apart. Don had been at Maxine's bedside, holding her hand, right to the end. Four hours after Maxine took her final breath, Don also died. One of the grandchildren said, "All Don wanted was to be with his beautiful wife. He adored my grandmother, loved her to the end of the Earth."

If there is a benevolent heart condition, indeed, takotsubo cardiomyopathy is the one. Yet, as the medical people state, people do not always die, but the emotional pain that they carry often makes death appear an attractive option. I am a journalist by trade, and it makes me almost feel like a war correspondent, surrounded by destruction and the smell of corpses. But I have not died; something far worse has happened. I have entered my own personal hell.

You may think I am overplaying my hand with the word 'hell', but not by a wide margin, I can assure you. For example, I frequently woke up in the middle of the night for several months, sobbing my eyes out. I was not having nightmares, and no thoughts were going through my sleeping brain as far as I was aware, but my soul was weeping. Sometimes, even today, over a year after the separation, my misery is so acute that when I awaken from a night's sleep, I feel a sensation that can only be described as shock or post-traumatic stress, which carries on throughout the day. It is often hard to function. On occasion, dark thoughts of 'quitting the game' run fleetingly through my head, and at such times I frequently feel the 'electricity' of my monastic guide.

My analogy to hell goes deeper, though. TDC messages such as *"We cannot help you in the fire"* and *"You'll step through the fire"* quickly bring to mind the home of the damned. As I listened to these TDCs, I did begin to wonder. The fire metaphor used by those in spirit certainly points to this possibility. However, I was quickly told that this was not the case: *"The fires of hell won't find you."*

Nevertheless, I have received several messages linked to 'The pain will go on forever' experience, including, *"The pain with you will not die off."* When I asked my guide about this and why the current problems had arisen, he replied puzzlingly, *"You're married; there lies a mystery."*

I had one further visit from the loneliness, the abyss, the same unbearable feeling I had in March 1983. The loneliness has never really gone away since the separation, but it is so much more intense when faced with the abyss - like the difference between being threatened with a gun and being shot.

The most recent of these occurred the evening before the first anniversary of the separation. I was listening to a piece of music, Gustav Mahler's Ninth Symphony. Now, I realise that many people will know nothing about this magnificent work, so I'll keep it simple. The last movement of this symphony has long been believed to portray death and the sadness that life is almost over. Mahler was seriously ill with a heart problem, and many commentators have, I now believe, put two and two together and come up with five.

As I was listening to the music, I began to feel a little odd. It was like I had taken half a step out of my body; I felt disorientated and a bit fearful of what was happening.

Then I began to tremble before the spiritual loneliness hit me hard. And in the few seconds I was experiencing this, I realised that Mahler's Ninth Symphony was not about death. It was about loneliness. Just as Catherine and Josie had done thirty-eight years previously, I burst into uncontrollable sobbing – I had entered the abyss. It only lasted for a few seconds, but it was horrible.

I then realised why this symphony was about loneliness. Alma, Mahler's wife, was the love of his life. He worshipped her, even writing down at one stage, 'To live for you, to die for you'. Yet Alma, a socialite and, it was said, one of the most beautiful women in Vienna, was unfaithful and, although she was there for Mahler towards the end of his life, she wasn't really 'there'. There are passages in Mahler's symphonies that are plainly about Alma, and I now believe that this one can be added to that list. I recall seeing the late Claudio Abbado, former music director of the Berlin Philharmonic and one of the finest interpreters of Mahler's music, explaining how deeply the great man loved his wife, concluding, "But she didn't understand." I have always felt a deep affinity with Mahler, but now even more so.

And this affinity became even deeper after I encountered another piece of Mahler's music that genuinely touched my soul. I had heard this music hundreds of times before, but on 1 June 2021, it 'exploded inside of me' in a way I could never have imagined and in a manner I find very difficult to explain. Nevertheless, shortly after the experience, I wrote my thoughts down.

Here, I ask the reader to try and go a little further than just the words; in fact, quite a lot further, because for me, what I am about to describe is very spiritual. It is based upon acceptance of what has happened, and I would go as far as to say that it forms the core of this book. These thoughts and words are the sun around which everything else revolves. It involves going into the pain and finding beauty at its heart. It's about unconditional love – it's about finding God.

"I have done everything that I came to do – love a wonderful woman unconditionally. It didn't end well, but that wasn't her fault, and it wasn't mine, either. In any event, I have lost her. And after you have loved so completely, there is nothing left to do, nowhere to go.

"All the same, I still needed to find some catharsis, and, as with other dreadful experiences in my life, I turned to music. I needed to find the musical equivalent of my pain – a work that I could fully lose myself in, something that is unbearably painful and unbearably beautiful, both at the same time. To find some kind of respite, I needed to square the circle.

"The last movement of Gustav Mahler's Tenth Symphony took me to that place. What had all of the warnings been about – the 'abyss' in 1983, the Amfortas Wound in 2020, the spirit voices, the whole spiritual panoply? I found all of the answers in this music. As I listened, I felt a pain I never thought possible and absolute bliss in the same second. This is love! If you truly love another person, with all of their faults and imperfections, that's what God is – you can touch the divine."

Turning Down the Dream

"The show must go on
The show must go on, yeah
Inside my heart is breaking
My makeup may be flaking
But my smile, still, stays on"
  Queen: The Show Must Go On

Love is the ultimate outlaw. It won't adhere to any rules, and no one can tame it. It's easy to love but to love someone despite everything, to know their flaws and love those too, that is rare and untainted and absolute.

In Leo Tolstoy's Anna Karenina, the heroine states: "Love. The reason I dislike that word is that it means too much for me, far more than you can understand." This is a good approximation of how I feel, so what can be done about it? People tell me that time is a great healer. It's not. People tell me that she wasn't worth it and to get on with life. She is, and I can't, no matter how hard I try. People tell me to start dating, meet someone else and my memories of her will soon fade. I did try this, although, from the beginning, it did seem a bit of a struggle, even though in normal circumstances (before I met my wife), Kate could well have been my perfect woman.

I have wanted to live in Italy for all my adult life, as I had done for a short time in my younger days, and have come close to doing so several times, only for life to intervene. So you'd think I would be more than happy to meet an attractive woman whose daughter lived in Turin and wanted her to move out there. "Is that something you'd consider?" she enquired with a nervous laugh. I just stared at her, my gaze drawn to the Nordic blue of her eyes. I liked Kate. She had honey-coloured hair and a deep, dusty voice, and she was entertaining, intelligent, and adventurous. Kate was also 16 years younger than me, something that many guys my age would look upon as something akin to a lottery win.

So there I was, sitting opposite a gorgeous woman who wanted to whisk me off to the land of my dreams. And what did I do? I found myself saying: "Sorry, I don't think that would be fair on you. I still love my wife." This lady was enchanting, but my wife is extraordinary.

I questioned Spirit about this admittedly short relationship and received the following TDC message, which was honest and supportive: *"Listen, it's the winter now ... a lot of pain, Roderick Millington ... you love Diane so much, it's hard to live now ... but you have faith ... you love her with all of your heart ... it's love, it's got a purpose."*

I must give the nod towards another woman, 'Tracy', who was introduced to me in August 2020 through TDC: *"Tracy will come and help you."* Tracy is the most phenomenal psychic medium and life coach. I had seen a therapist to help me get through this period and, although she was excellent, she only had temporal answers, and the relationship ran out of steam. I needed more, which is how I came across Tracy a couple of weeks after Christmas 2020.

This, of course, was during the lockdown, so we spoke on the telephone. As soon as she introduced herself, I felt spiritual electricity flow through my body, and it continued to do so for the remaining 40 minutes of this first session.

Before starting any serious work, Tracy insisted on giving me a reading and told me I must remain quiet until it was over – she didn't want to know anything about me. Her accuracy was stunning. She began by telling me: "I need to say to you in the relationship situation, it brings tears, it stings my eyes, so for me, it's on that level, I want to breathe with it, but I can't."

This was followed, a few minutes later, by: "There's a lady who has just come in from Spirit, and I do feel as if it's a grandmother link. She's the sort of lady who just got on with it, scrubbed the steps. She's quite formidable; Ida or Ivy, something with that kind of sound." My grandmother, on my father's side, was Ivy.

She then said something that could tie in with the fire motifs in this story, including the monks getting burned. "She's (Diane) actually a really nice person. But there's some parental stuff that went on that wasn't very nice. I need to give you that. And I need to say to you that you've been in different lifetimes together, but I feel that ... and I do need to say to you there was ... I don't know ... she was burned, or there was some stuff with that, but there are some real issues there. But they are just making me aware of stuff that's gone on in the past that plays a part in this lifetime too."

Tracy then asked, "Who is Diane please?" And almost immediately after, "Who's the 'F' in Spirit who wants to say hello to you – is it Fred or Frank." I replied, "That would be Fred," but didn't say who he was. Tracy continued: Ah, right, he's saying, "You've got this, son." Fred was my father.

Everything she said was making sense; indeed, a lot she was saying about Diane was making complete sense, which on a deep level was helping me to cope with the situation. It's been several months since that first chat with Tracy, and I'm still feeling a tremendous spiritual upliftment. It was not only what she said; it was something more nebulous – maybe that's why I was feeling the electricity, what she was saying was true.

Before Tracy ended the reading, she stated the following: "You're inspired by somebody as well. You see, I haven't got a religious bone in my body, so that doesn't help, but they're showing me somebody supports you. He's a priest or a monk, and he is brutal! There is absolutely no way you won't do this (work more with and write about Spirit). It's as though they'll take everything away from you until you do. He's definitely guiding you. Just keep asking him to show you what are you doing next? But what they're showing me is as clear as day. I need to say that you love your partner more than anyone, but she just doesn't get it. How sad." And I instantly recalled Claudio Abbado talking about Gustav Mahler and realised that Mahler too carried the Amfortas Wound.

In this lifetime, I have learned how to love completely. I refuse to become angry. I'm not going to make the world any better by shouting at it. It's true, with the 'Amfortas Wound', I am in emotional pain all of the time. But if I gave in to it, I would do nothing. I don't regret a moment of my time with Diane – a ship is safe in harbour, but that's not what ships are for, so I sailed to the far horizon and found a woman who gave my life meaning. And that is the greatest gift I have ever received.

The show must go on.

Travelling in Time

"No, there was nothing unusual in any of these dreams as dreams. They were merely displaced in Time."
J.W. Dunne, Experiment with Time

I have mentioned several dreams throughout this book, some precognitive, others seemingly residing in another realm. But the one conclusion I have reached regarding dreams is that once in the arms of Morpheus, it is possible to time travel. It's like having your own tiny Tardis. In other words, the head that hits the pillow might be relatively small physically, but it's bigger on the inside.

The first time I recall having a precognitive dream was when I was just six years of age. At that time, I used to play on the motorway. I had better explain that. I was born and raised in England's second city, Birmingham, close to an M6 construction site. My friends and I used to visit the site regularly – it was often flooded, and we used to take rafts out onto the fast lane! Actually, it was just a hole in the ground, but I knew what was coming.

I had a very clear dream that has stayed with me for the rest of my life, where I am standing on the road that now crosses the M6 motorway at Junction 7, the main road from Birmingham to Walsall. When I had the dream, the site was still primarily fields, a bluebell wood, and an old quarry. In the dream, though, I saw the entire finished project, including the bridge, motorway, off and on-ramps, and associated roadways. I now realise that I was time travelling, for my dream was perfect in every detail.

Of course, being a dream, it also got a bit weird. As I looked up from the bridge, I saw the planet Mercury heading towards the Moon, which, I somehow realised, would be hit in a snooker ball-like fashion, sending the latter hurtling towards Earth.

Instantaneously, I found myself on the corner of a road a couple of hundred yards away. I was standing in front of a house with an old Anderson Shelter in the garden. There was also a hearse parked outside, which I first noticed as I began to walk up the path to the front door. Once inside the house, I found myself in a small room with a curtain separating it from an adjoining room. Then I heard a voice proclaim: "You can walk through the curtain into a past-life, or you can stay here and witness the end of the world." I chose to walk through the curtain and found myself in what I intuitively knew was 19th-century America, complete with rolling wheat fields and a small homestead. This is where the dream ended.

Yet, apparently, although unknown to me until much later, I had American connections even earlier in my life.

The first few years of my life were relatively uneventful. At least I assume they were; I am unable to recollect anything of those early times. My very first memory was as a four-year-old sitting on the living room carpet, delighted that my father had brought a kitten home, initially pretending that the box he was carrying contained coal. But in that same year, something else happened that I do not remember, but my mother did.

I was playing in the 'box room'. I have no idea what I was playing, but I was by myself. However, my mother informed me that she heard singing and came and stood outside of the room and listened for a few minutes. She felt goosebumps, so she said, as the realisation came over her as to exactly what it was I was singing - old American songs; one, in particular, my mother heard in the 1930s when she was just a child herself.

I asked her several times over the years if she could recall the titles of the songs. She could not, except to say that one was about a campground, but she had never heard that song before. She did remember that I appeared to be performing these two or three songs word perfect and could not understand where I could have heard them, let alone learned the words.

It was not until 2015 that I may have discovered what the campground song was. One of my big passions in life is music, and I found not too long before Christmas a CD entitled '1865 - Songs of Hope and Home from the American Civil War' by Anonymous 4. I read the review of this CD maybe a year earlier but had not seen a complete track listing or heard any of the songs. Then one day, whilst trawling on Amazon, I came across the album and sound clips of all of the songs. Track 7 was 'Tenting on the Old Camp Ground'. Now it would make a great story if I could say that I recognised the song straight away and began to sing along without a lyric sheet. I didn't. It was just a song on an album I had not heard, like countless other songs.

I have had quite a few dreams about the United States through the years; several of them unusual, but none that could be called 'psychic'. In the autumn of 2015, though, I did reencounter the American Civil War when a TDC voice spoke to me clearly with the words: *"Passed the guns of Eltham."* This was conveyed at the same time I was explaining the motorway dream to three friends. Now I didn't know where or what Eltham was, so I did what everyone now does when they have a question they can't answer; I Googled it, and this is what Wikipedia had to say:

"The Battle of Eltham's Landing, also known as the Battle of Barhamsville, or West Point, took place on 7 May 1862, in New Kent County, Virginia, as part of the Peninsula Campaign of the American Civil War. Brigadier General William B Franklin's Union division landed at

Eltham's Landing. It was attacked by two brigades of Brigadier General GW Smith's command, reacting to the threat to the Confederate army's trains on the Barhamsville Road. Franklin's movement occurred while the Confederate army was withdrawing from the Williamsburg line, but he was unable to interfere with the Confederate movement.' It also says that The Battle at Eltham's Landing was little more than a heavy skirmish. There were 194 Union casualties and 48 Confederate."

But that wasn't the end of it. Quite out of the blue, several days after the dream, my psychic medium friend, Pauline, said to me, "I have 'seen' a drummer boy, and it gave me a strange feeling because I thought it was you." Then she gave me another two names: Mr Palmer (pseudonym) and Franklin.

Drummer boys served a critically important purpose on the battlefield during the American Civil War. They had to learn dozens of drum calls, and the playing of each call would tell the soldiers they were required to perform a specific task. When the fighting began, drummers generally moved to the rear and stayed away from the shooting. However, Civil War battlefields were dangerous places, and drummers were known to be killed or wounded.

After a bit of research, and with the Eltham TDC in mind, I discovered a possible candidate – a Jack Thomas Palmer who had spent much of his life in a small town in Illinois. This immediately caught my attention because back in my teens, I had a dream I have always remembered where I was in Chicago and heard a loud voice proclaim, "You must go to Illinois." I never did, but dreams of being in America have been a constant in my life, maybe one or two a year.

I began to dig deeper into the Jack Thomas Palmer story and discovered several fascinating facts, not least

125

that he was born on 8 April 1845 in Franklin, Pennsylvania. I then found out that he enlisted in the 64th Illinois Voluntary Infantry on 22 March 1860, after four years serving as a drummer boy.

One of the things to look out for when researching past lives is 'number patterns'; that is, numbers that reoccur from life to life, but in different circumstances. I got married on 22 March, while as a youngster, perhaps between the ages of five and seven, I was obsessed with the number sixty-four. Eventually, I brought it down to sixteen because sixty-four was too big to handle in an OCD sense. Because that's what it was, OCD – I was genuinely fixated on that number. During the same period, I also used to go round playing drum rolls with my lips. I recall my mother saying to me, "Your lips will get stuck like that if you don't stop!" I still subconsciously carry out several other Americanisms too. Until the age of about twenty-five, for instance, I was still asking for the 'check' in restaurants instead of the bill. I still do it sometimes, but I don't always notice.

Jack Thomas Palmer participated in many civil war battles, including the Siege of Corinth and the Battles of Columbus Creek, Iuka, Glendale, Resaca, Kingston and Big Shanty. He was also with General Sherman on his famous March to the Sea. Still, I could find no mention of the Battle of Eltham. That does not mean it didn't occur; Palmer was in many battles and skirmishes.

Discharged in Chicago on 28 July 1865, Palmer travelled considerably in his life, making four trips to California and back. And, as a farmer, he undoubtedly made trips to visit various clients. I mention this because of one more dream I had. I was on a train, and it was snowing. What's more, while on the train, I also hovered high above it (the kind of thing that can only happen in dreams), looking down at the railway track as it curved around and back on itself to pull into what I knew was St Louis railway station. Naturally, I did some checking and, while the station no longer exists – it is now a shopping mall – I discovered that the track curves around precisely the same as in the dream. Moreover, the roof of the station was identical to the roof in my dream. And the cherry on the cake – there were trains where he lived to St Louis, and farmers used to travel to the city to do business.

One final thing when considering the Jack Thomas Palmer link is that, while researching, I used to meet with a small group who were fascinated with such subjects. One of this group, Linda, was very interested in the whole Illinois connection. When I found Palmer's 21st-century family on Facebook, I came across a picture of his great-great-granddaughter, who was Linda's double. I showed it to another friend and asked who it was? "That's Linda," she replied, a little puzzled as to why I was asking such a daft question. So, was Linda there too? I wouldn't rule it out.

The Jack Thomas Palmer potential past life does not prove anything, but it continues a theme that began over fifty years ago. And sometimes, if it looks like an elephant, it probably is an elephant. Consequently, I have to keep an open mind.

As a result, the motorway dream appeared to be looking forward and backwards in time – the building of Junction 7 and a previous incarnation in America.

It seems that precognitive dreams can foretell things years in advance or, in the following example, events that are mere hours away. It was the summer of 2001, and for some reason, I woke up feeling quite stressed after dreaming of a car accident – I was driving down an empty road when a tractor pulled out in front of me. I screamed, hit it, and the dream ended. I didn't want to drive that day but had to attend a meeting, so I set off. About two miles from home, on an empty stretch of road, I was travelling at around 50mph when suddenly, out of nowhere, a car pulled out in from on me. I had to brake hard, putting my vehicle into a spin, bouncing off the kerb and coming to a halt pointing in the wrong direction. The other car stopped, and the driver walked over to see if I was okay. As he reached me, the smell of alcohol was overpowering. I was warned, it seems, but it's hard to gauge how I could have done anything about the incident.

A couple of years later, I had a dream where my cousin, Dean, left his body. Later that day, I found myself on a mile-long walk down a country lane to buy myself a Sunday newspaper. At this time, Dean was critically ill in hospital. He had contracted a very rare form of cancer, located initially in the spine but now spread to other areas of the body, including the brain. Dean had been in hospital for two or three months and, as I was walking, I recalled the dream and wondered how long he could survive? With that thought, I heard a loud male voice say, "May the sixteenth". Dean died a few days later, on 16 May.

Another warning dream the following year concerned the death of my father. He was not a well man, but there was no imminent sign of his passing. However, around two weeks before he did pass, I had a dream that, in retrospect, I realise was telling me what was going to happen. Neeme Järvi, a famous orchestral conductor, had died, and I saw his two sons, also orchestral conductors, standing next to a graveside. I have an older brother, and soon my father's two sons would be standing next to a graveside. Sometimes a little interpretation is needed with dreams.

Another dream, the night before my father went into a coma, informed me that the end was near. I found myself in a boxing ring with Mike Tyson, and my father was in my corner. I knew there was no escaping and that once

Iron Mike hit me, it would be excruciating. When I awoke, I instinctively knew what the dream was about, and it was no surprise when, roughly six hours later, my mother called to say that my father could not get out of bed. I phoned for an ambulance, and later that night, in Walsall Manor Hospital, he fell into a coma. He remained in this state for a week, but I knew it was already a technical knock-out.

It's not always bad news. Sometimes dreams can announce important events that will happen weeks, months or even years in advance.

It was 1992, and I worked as the editor of a group of business magazines in Hull, but the publishing company that employed me went out of business. Naturally, I was concerned about what would happen next. During this time, I dreamed of walking around the Jewellery Quarter district in Birmingham, where I worked for a short time after leaving school. It was a very clear, lucid dream, which saw me walk into an industrial unit on the corner of a road. There were several different rooms within this building, but all of them were empty. Then I heard a booming, distinctive voice that said, "This is Eddie's place; it's not ready yet - wait a few years."

Three years later, in the summer of 1995, I met Eddie, working alongside him at a publishing company in Leeds. However, in September 1997, he broke away to form his own business. He asked if my company would provide his new business with all of the copy for the various magazines they intended to publish. I took a gamble and said yes. Today, twenty-four years later, I still provide all of the copy for their magazines, but since 2004 they have been based in Dubai, so my 'patch' nowadays tends to be the United Arab Emirates, Saudi Arabia, Qatar, Oman, Kuwait, and Bahrain. This, it seems, was all foreseen around three years before I met Eddie and five years before he first launched his business.

I started dating my wife, Diane, in 2002. I'd been given a few 'clues' about her, though, two or three months before we first met. Of course, I didn't realise they were clues at the time, but looking back, they now seem blindingly obvious. A plan was unfolding.

One spring evening, I went to bed early after a hectic day and fell into a deep sleep. I had a dream; actually, it wasn't much of a dream, merely a map of Africa just hanging in space. There were no details on this map, it was jet black, but it was very recognisable as the 'dark continent'.

A few nights later, I had the first of a series of dreams where a 2/3 motif kept repeating itself. Most of these dreams were about football matches: in one, I was leaving Villa Park in Birmingham, and I looked up at the scoreboard, which read Aston Villa 2 West Bromwich Albion 3. I thought at first that this was just a wish fulfilment dream; then the next night I had another dream where I was reading a newspaper: the headline read Arsenal 2 Manchester City 3. A couple of days later, this was followed by another dream that involved the scoreline Celtic 2 Inverness 3. In all, there were five dreams with the 2/3 motif in the space of a couple of weeks.

The first time I met Diane, I discovered that she had recently returned from South Africa after twenty-seven years, and when I visited her home, I found myself exiting junction 23 of the M1 motorway. It all smacked of pre-arrangement.

I have one other link to Africa and, although not a dream, it is pertinent to this book. I was born in a 1930s semi-detached house in Birmingham, England. I arrived bang on time, a trait that I still possess today and which admittedly does irritate some people. As I was 'making my entrance', my grandmother re-entered the room (I don't know where she had been), stopped suddenly in her tracks, and proclaimed, "Who is that big black man?" My mother and father related this story to me many years later, as did the grandmother in question. Once I had emerged and been slapped, she described to my parents a very tall African warrior in full ceremonial dress observing the birth.

Have I ever felt an affinity for Africa? No, not really. Even so, if my grandmother is to be believed, and I have no reason to question her story – she was a very straightforward, down-to-earth woman – I did have an African warrior at my birth. There is nothing more to say on the subject of the African warrior, except that he appears to have been my spiritual maternity nurse!

Some precognitive dreams have an additional, mystical aspect to them. For example, Derek and I shared a passion for music and hung out together regularly during our teens and early twenties. Unfortunately, in 1975, his father became unwell, although there was no suggestion that his number would be called anytime soon.

Nevertheless, in a very lucid dream state, I stood in the lounge with him, telling him quite calmly that he had passed away but that everything would be okay. I recall he was dressed in a burgundy patterned dressing gown and seemed very distressed and bewildered. He didn't want to accept that he was dead, his eyes showing the tortured dullness of disbelief. Out of the blue, the door from the lounge to the hallway opened, and there was a brilliant white light, out of which stepped two people, one woman and one man, donning white robes and carrying flowers. Their faces were full of strength, shining with a steadfast and serene peace. Without looking at me, they said, "We'll take over now. Thank you." The dream ended abruptly.

The following day, which was a Saturday, Derek and I were meant to be playing football for a local team and were due to meet at around 9.30 am. At roughly 8.30 am, though, he telephoned me to say that he wouldn't be coming that day; his father had died. Through TDC, Spirit later told me, *"You have a link with Heaven."* Well, I certainly did on that day.

An intriguing follow-up to this story took place maybe ten years later when I was flicking through a book featuring photographs of ghosts. One, in particular, caught my attention. There were a couple of dozen people standing around the grave at a funeral. Almost all were dressed soberly; lots of suits, black ties, and hats. Yet, one figure stood out. He was wearing a long white robe and looked very similar to the people I had seen in the 'dream'. No one at the funeral had seen this man. Although why anyone was taking a photograph of a funeral, to begin with, I have no idea! However, I must point out that this photograph was taken before the advent of Photoshop, before the development of personal computers, back in the days when the old saying 'the camera never lies' could be taken at face value.

The death of Derek's father and the fact that I appeared to have somehow been there had a massive impact on me – it opened up my mind to all kinds of possibilities.

As you might expect, I have also enjoyed a handful of 'Jesus dreams'.

The first I remember, in my early twenties, is one where I found myself in a cave with a three-times life-size statue of Jesus lit up in blue. What did this signify? I have no idea. But other dreams followed, all equally as perplexing. Then I started to feel a 'pull', a calling. At the age of twenty-two, I was considering joining the priesthood. In the end, I didn't because I was afraid of what family and friends would say, and I think I missed a genuine calling.

I must point out at this stage, though, that I was a very typical youngster in so many ways. I went to football matches, attended numerous concerts by bands such as Thin Lizzy and The Who, drank copious amounts of beer (and other types of liquid refreshment), and discovered women. Not just 'girls', having a torrid affair with a thirty-year-old mother of two when I was only twenty-one. This is important. I was no angel. It was a life of sex and drink and rock n' roll. I even ran away to work overseas on several occasions, in Italy, Spain, and Greece, where the aforementioned 'vices' became turbo-charged. And yet, throughout all of this, I felt a pull towards a more spiritual life, a more meaningful life.

The next Jesus dream I will mention found me travelling in an open-top car, sitting in the rear and feeling the wind against my face. There was a chauffeur upfront, complete with uniform and peaked cap. As I looked to my right, I could see we were moving past a grassy incline and, at the top, about twenty yards or so, I would guess, was a brick wall around twelve feet high. The car suddenly ground to a halt. I immediately saw a relatively steep set of steps, which led up to an open gateway in the wall. "If you want to speak to Jesus, he is at the top of the steps, just inside the gateway," my chauffeur announced. I felt ecstatic; this was a fantastic opportunity, so I climbed out of the car and started to make my way up the steps. I was approximately three-quarters of the way up when I began to feel unsure, and then I realised that if I stood in front of Christ at this time, I would quite literally explode from the energy he would be giving out. I could sense that energy. Consequently, I turned around and made my way back down to the car. I'd bottled it!

I awoke immediately after this dream with a jolt, and I could feel spiritual electricity flowing through my body. I could still sense the power of Christ. I could hardly breathe.

Several years later, I had my next Jesus dream, and this time I 'almost' got to speak to him! I was walking in a kind of procession across a large, flat piece of land close to a town; I could see the houses and street lights in the distance, perhaps a mile away. The whole area was laid mainly to lawn, but we followed a paved path, around thirty of us, with someone leading the way with a flaming torch. About two hundred yards in front of us, we could see Jesus walking the same path, dressed in white robes and an archetypal beard and long hair.

Now, strange to say that in this dream, I remembered the last dream. I recalled that I couldn't go through with it and backed away from my chance to speak to Jesus. I was determined not to make the same mistake this time! So I bucked up my courage and ran ahead of the group towards Him. As I reached Him, we had come to a short (maybe one hundred yards) tunnel, much like the underpasses seen in most British towns and cities from the 1960s – it was constructed in concrete and had no redeeming architectural qualities whatsoever. I was walking close to him when he lifted his hand and 'threw' a fireball down the tunnel. I have no idea what this aspect of the dream was about. He began to walk through the tunnel, and I followed just a few feet behind. When we came out into the fresh air again, I finally found the courage to run up and walk alongside him, and I had a fundamental question to ask.

Unfortunately, I can't remember what the question was. However, just as I was about to speak, Jesus stopped to turn into a doorway. But before stepping through the door,

He looked at me and said, "Go to the restaurant where all the food is free." Then He was gone.

Again, I woke up with a jolt and felt spiritual electricity surging very strongly through my entire being. But what could 'go to the restaurant where all the food is free' mean? I have a theory.

Today, religion and spirituality have become an industry – a big industry. From the Catholic Church raking in millions from property and stocks and shares through to some pretty dubious New Age disciplines, spirituality has been hijacked by charlatans and entrepreneurs. If you want to go to Heaven, have a mystical experience, or be healed, you are going to hand over a fair bit of cash. I believe that what Jesus was saying in the dream was that spirituality is your divine right; it's what you are; you do not have to pay anyone an admittance fee. When he was healing, Jesus never sent out invoices.

Time travel is not limited to dreams either. There are instances in day to day life when we travel through time, but no one notices. There are two such occurrences in my life, for example, to do with my love of music.

It was August 1975, and I was on holiday on the Spanish island of Mallorca. Walking along the seafront one morning, I saw a newspaper billboard outside of a shop that proclaimed, 'Shostakovich Dead'. At the time, I had no idea who Shostakovich was, but that billboard seared itself into my memory for reasons I couldn't readily understand for many years. However, Shostakovich has become a massive part of my life – his music has helped me get through many challenging situations; he has almost been like a therapist, always there when I need him.

It's the same with Gustav Mahler. This incident was slightly different in context, but it still seared itself into my memory. I was walking past a music store in

Birmingham called Hudson's, and in the window was a display revolving around a new vinyl record that had been released. There were album covers, cut-outs, all advertising Simon Rattle and the Bournemouth Symphony Orchestra performing Mahler's Tenth Symphony. Again, I didn't know who Mahler was, and I had no genuine interest in the display as such, yet it has stayed in my memory as if it was yesterday for over forty years. And Mahler, like Shostakovich, has been a massive part of my life and musical education.

There have been many more psychic dreams and time travelling events down the years, and the story continues to evolve even as I am writing this book. As the old maxim goes, you live and learn. Well, you live anyway.

Good Morning, this is Heaven!

"We may be surprised at the people we find in Heaven. God has a soft spot for sinners. His standards are quite low."
  Desmond Tutu

Demonstrating the existence of God can be somewhat tricky, a fact acknowledged by Spirit. In one instance, during a TDC session, a Christian woman asked how she could prove God to friends. The response was simple and to the point: *"Lady, you cannot prove God."* On another occasion, when someone asked whether Jesus was in Heaven, we were told, *"He's here, and God's near him."* Other messages seem to back up humankind's long-held ideas of a creator and where this creator resides: *"God has loved you forever,"* and *"Here there is a sense of God."* In this last message, the 'here' was Heaven, for we had already heard the statement: *"I can reach, this is her, Heaven calling."*

The term 'Heaven' traditionally refers to the spirit realm, a level of existence higher than and outside of the physical universe. Of course, everyone wants to know about Heaven, and everyone wants to go there. But does it exist? Increasing evidence suggests that it does. Leading brain surgeon Dr Eben Alexander, for example, has written about his experiences of Heaven during the time he was clinically dead during an illness.

It is interesting to note that on many occasions, the TDC voices ask us to try to recall where we are originally from, which they say can be achieved through prayer and meditation, depending on one's spiritual path: *"We want you to remember Heaven."*

One of the cheeriest greetings I have ever received during TDC sessions was a voice that instantly announced, *"Good morning, this is Heaven!"*

Messages can be very personal, too. We can be called by name, such as in the following message I received from my mother: *"Heaven is a place, Rick ... we're in Heaven; you're still my boy."*

So if there is a place called Heaven, could there be beings we term angels, too?

It's a nice thought, I admit, that we might all have our own personal guardian angel. Because unlike many of the people I seem to be speaking with nowadays, I'm still very much alive. But there is one small problem with life - nothing at all works. The roads don't work, the trains don't work, and I've been marooned at more airports than I care to remember. So a guardian angel would be lovely.

But what about angels such as Michael and Raphael, the big hitters, because I've always thought of guardian angels as more like spirit guides, with the title 'angel' being honorary.

The term 'angel' comes from the Greek word 'angelos', which is equivalent to the Hebrew word mal'akh, meaning 'messenger'. Originally, they were seen as fearless warriors, both in Heaven in the war against Lucifer and on Earth. Warrior angels, for instance, defeated the Assyrians.

Those who claim to have been in the presence of angels also state quite firmly that they are neither male nor female but androgynous. The fine detail depends on your religion. Early Christians borrowed the Cherubim and Seraphim from the Old Testament, as well as the notion of a hierarchy (Dominions, Virtues, Archangels, etc.). Jews have been vague on ranking angels. Christians have made a science out of it.

Today, hundreds of stores specialise in angel paraphernalia, selling everything from soap in the shape of wings to cherubim incense. I even hear that the sale of harps has gone up. Angels today, it seems, are adorable little creatures with a gigantic wingspan. What's more, they are more than happy to spend their time searching the streets for a parking space - one of the little things angelologists tell us we should ask angels for instead of bothering God.

In their modern incarnation, these once-powerful messengers and fearless soldiers have been relegated to a position of subservience. It is nice to have angels available as readily as paracetamol for those who find God and his rules just a tad uncompromising. They're non-threatening, insightful and considerate. They work in God's PR department and are ready and waiting whenever we call.

Only in the so-called 'New Age' is it possible to have angels that can be totally ignored unless we're desperate for help. And I mean desperate. Then they turn up with a sweet smile and a magic wand. Yet, according to the world's holy books, anyone who has an encounter with an angel is changed forever. In the Book of Daniel, we find an angel 'clothed in linen, whose loins were girded with fine gold of Uphaz. His body also was like beryl, and his face as the appearance of lightning, and his eyes as lamps of fire, and his arms and his feet like in colour to polished brass, and the voice of his words like the voice of a multitude'. In the Book of Revelation, angels do battle with a dragon. In modern-day Cardiff, they'll find you a parking space.

And if all that were not enough, these 'angelologists' will, for a small donation, put you in touch with your guardian angel. They are all around you, this strange breed of New Age professionals will tell you. Still, it feels considerably more pleasant to be on the alert for angels, as opposed to, say, muggers.

As many children will tell you who have had a near-death experience, though - admittedly with a tad of disgust - angels do not have wings! In an age where more and more people turn to angels in the same way they turn to Citizens Advice, it takes a child to bring us all back down to Earth. As one little girl noted, "They don't look like people, and we can't see them. When they come down-to-earth, they take a form that people won't object to."

William Barrett, Professor of Physics at the Royal College of Science in Dublin in the early part of the 20th century, made several observations concerning his own dying patients' final days and hours in a booklet entitled Deathbed Visions. Many times at the moment of death, he noted, people would see a friend or relative at their bedside whom they believed to be alive. In all cases, when it was checked out, however, it was discovered that the person they saw had died before them without their knowledge. Professor Barrett also reported that dying children often expressed considerable surprise that the angels they saw waiting for them did not have wings.

Despite this, I still had terrible difficulty believing in angels. If it weren't simply the logic of the situation that disturbed me, it certainly would have been that New Agers treated them like little puppies. So I had trouble with the concept of the planet being guided by beings from a loving angelic realm.

Then I did a TDC session.

I'd heard myself saying, "I don't believe in angels. Yet who is he? If there really is someone watching over me, where does he come from?" Playing this sentence back and putting it through the TDC process, I discovered that where I said, "Yet who is he?" there was a very clear example of TDC that stated quite simply, *"He is your angel."*

Ah, that I didn't expect. And it was backed up a month or so later when I visited a pub with a friend. That evening, there were several psychic mediums giving sittings to raise money for charity. My friend invested ten pounds and was told, well, absolutely nothing that made sense. However, he had recorded the session, so I suggested looking for TDCs so that his money wouldn't be entirely wasted. The first message I got was from the medium's own soul: *"I'm making this up."* No real surprise there. But it was the second message from a spirit that made me take a step backwards: *"No respect towards the angels."*

I was going to have to rethink my entire outlook when it came to angels, which was underlined around a year later when discussing someone who was in trouble in a health sense, both mentally and physically. *"The house of the angels will come and help,"* was the TDC message I received.

Oh well, you can't be right all the time.

Many spiritual seekers seem to think of God as a self-serve buffet, mixing and matching different facets of several religions to fit an acceptable mould, which is probably how angels have morphed. There is sound reasoning behind this. God is too big to fit into any single faith. Genuine spirituality is much more than religion, an observance, or belief in God. It is at the core of what produces the yearning for a belief in something else in the universe. It is our souls reaching out.

'Inner' Christianity is my path and has been, so it seems, for many lifetimes. It may not be yours, of course, and that's okay. As Jesus said, "In my father's house, there are many mansions."

There are several reasons I am a Christian. In the summer of 2017, for instance, I became anxious about a particular person and was worried about the outcome of her actions. So I prayed. I suppose not in the usual way; instead, I walked around my lounge for twenty minutes talking to Jesus. I didn't get an instant response (I didn't expect one) and went to bed feeling a little down.

Nonetheless, I awoke at around 2.00 am in a state of absolute bliss! It's hard to describe. I even got out of bed and went to the bathroom, still in an ecstatic state. After going back to bed, I woke up again at just turned 5.00 am, and I still felt blissful – it was magical. Finally, I got out of bed to prepare for the day ahead at 7.00 am, and the feeling had gone; I was back to 'normal'. Even so, I felt at peace and knew I wasn't on my own, and everything would be okay. Prayer does work.

Psalm 46:10 immediately sprang to mind when this event occurred: 'Be still and know that I am God'. And I suppose that 'my God' is a kind, caring, creative being, not the lunatic described in a fair chunk of the Old Testament and worshipped by King James.

The King James Bible, long celebrated as one of the most significant texts of all time, provides first-rate reasons for tracking down and killing witches. Traditional images of witches portray them as ugly, hook-nosed women in league with the devil. However, history tells us that the real story is far less disturbing. In reality, those women considered to be witches were healers and respected members of their communities. They made house calls, delivered babies, and treated the sick. But the image of a knowledgeable and loving woman was changed into an evil figure appropriate for burning thanks to King James and others like him.

Matthew Hopkins, the infamous Witchfinder General, was believed to have been responsible for the execution of over 100 suspected witches between 1644 and 1646 alone. Why? Primarily because of Exodus 22:18: 'Thou shalt not suffer a witch to live'.

This seems a reasonably clear rule. But what hasn't been heeded is that the King James text was translated from Greek and Latin texts that had been translated from Hebrew and Aramaic before finally making it into the English language. That is cause enough for concern. It is reminiscent of the children's party game, where a short sentence is whispered to the youngster sitting adjacent. Then, a dozen or so children later, it comes out as a completely different statement – 'The train is late today' quickly becomes 'it will rain later today'.

Then, of course, we mustn't forget that some concepts and words do not translate well from one language to another. For example, in the original Greek, 'Thou shall not suffer a witch to live' reads, 'Thou shalt not suffer a venefica to live'. Ah, so 'venefica' is the Greek word for a witch? Er ... no. Venefica means 'female poisoner'. So the correct translation should be 'Thou shalt not suffer a female poisoner to live', which seems eminently more acceptable than hanging and burning women who lived close to nature and, in many instances, were the GPs of their local villages. But King James did the editing, and this incorrect and dangerous translation has now found its way into many other Bibles, which have equally ignorant editors and publishers.

King James and many other despots have mistranslated and abused the Bible to force the public to take on board their own often warped views. Innumerable instances of the King James Bible's mistranslations have now been set in stone and established as a fact for most Christians. But they are not; they are wrong and frequently hateful.

So why do most Christians believe that psychic mediums are in league with the devil? The answer is that the majority are ill-informed thanks to some pretty dodgy interpretation of the Bible over the past couple of thousand years, often by preachers and scholars who should know better.

The 'mediumship is evil' brigade often point to the Book of Leviticus for proof that psychics should be hung, drawn, and quartered. However, if they tried to follow the rules in this ancient text, they would soon be in trouble. Take Leviticus 19, for instance: 'Do not wear clothing woven of two kinds of material; Do not eat any meat with the blood still in it; Do not cut the hair at the sides of your head or clip off the edges of your beard; Do not cut your bodies for the dead or put tattoo marks on yourselves. I am the Lord.'

Taking just those four pronouncements into account means that several billion souls get consigned to the fiery depths of hell for eternity, which seems a bit harsh for trimming a beard. Then there are the commands God gave to kill adulterers, the LGBTQ community, and people who work on a Saturday (Leviticus 20:10; Leviticus 20:13; and Exodus 35:2, respectively). The Old Testament also gives the thumbs up to slavery, the rape of female captives in wartime, and child sacrifice. And my personal 'favourite', in Kings 2:23-24, is where God sends two bears out of the woods to tear forty-two children to pieces because they called someone names.

So my Christianity is informed rather than taking everything verbatim from the pulpit. And I am not someone whose faith is absolute; I too doubt. To quote Father Lucas, the Anthony Hopkins character in the film The Rite: "There are times when I experience a total loss of faith: days, months, when I don't know what I believe in, God, or the devil, Santa Claus or Tinkerbell. But I'm just a man. I'm a weak man. I have no power. Yet, there's something that keeps digging and scraping away inside me. Feels like God's fingernail. And finally, I can take no more of the pain, and I get shoved out from the darkness, back into the light."

I guess my religion is the same as the one Jesus preached – love. And that's why I call Jesus my Master. And it appears that whatever path you choose, love plays a significant part in where you go when you die.

There are many planes of existence, the 'top tier' (at the least the top one we can aspire to at our current stage of spiritual evolution) being what we call Heaven. Therefore, we will end with a message from Spirit that should point us all in the right direction in our current incarnations, and that is to do with love. Not lust, not even parental love, but agape, unconditional, divine love. That means no prejudices, no intolerance, and no judgement. It sounds a bit of a challenge sometimes, but one of the most important messages I have ever received from Heaven is: *"If you can't love, you can't go there."*

To hear a selection of TDC voices, please visit www.roderickmillington.co.uk

Printed in Great Britain
by Amazon